Flash Memoir:
Writing Prompts to Get You Flashing

Kitchen Sink Press 

Flash Memoir:
Writing Prompts to Get You Flashing

Jane Hertenstein

JANE HERTENSTEIN

Introduction

What sparks memory? Something as simple as a whiff of lilac can summon up a scene from our past. That one memory may lead to others, setting off a cascade until suddenly we are lost. Remembering can be a type of daydreaming—or for others self-torture from which they can never escape.

Thank God there are limits to memory.

With long-term memory we are able to reach back to a pool of memories. Be they collective or individual, there are things we simply know. Some of us, mostly husbands, are afflicted with short-term memory, the ability to hold a certain amount of information for only a short time.

Whether long or short, many of us contrive to retain a to-do list or study for tests or to order flowers for a special birthday. This is working memory.

Yet what about those memories which come to us unbidden, at the most inconvenient times, random, without logic? I call this flashing. Synapses set in motion or triggered by seemingly unrelated external prompts.

The five senses are some of the strongest agitators of memory. Recall Proust in *In Search of Lost Time* or also known as *Remembrance of Things Past* where he writes about involuntary memory instigated by a simple cookie. Dunking a tea biscuit can easily lead one on a journey into the past. Some call this nostalgia or déjà vu. Sometimes memories are aroused by conversation with another or with relatives around a table at Christmas time.

One thing is sure: We often have no control over what we remember or forget. Because of trauma some memories are suppressed or hidden until awoken by similar tragedy or uncovered by psychoanalysis.

Which leads us to false and true memories. *Total Recall* was the name of a science-fiction movie. No one has the ability of total recall. Always our memories will be challenged by objective reality, by others. My sister will remember the exact same event much differently than me. Her perspective can accommodate or lend another aspect to the event, or run completely counter. I am not a psychologist or neurologist, able to point out which lobes or parts of the brain are in charge of what, though I know the hippocampus is thought to be the center of memory—and emotion. Much of what we remember is emotionally charged. Anne Sexton is quoted as saying: "It doesn't matter who my father was; it matters who I remember he was."

Sometimes this is all we have, and we must begin there.

Flash is also a literary term, meaning short. Word counts vary, but generally flash is thought to be 1,000 words or less. Some journals in their submission guidelines can be very specific. *Smokelong* for instance asks for flash that can easily be consumed in the amount of time it takes to finish a cigarette. One journal may want 66 words while another request only 6, just read guidelines carefully. Flash is a form that can be applied to almost any genre. There are flash mysteries. Postcard flash might only be about travel—you are limited to the amount of space typically taken up by the back of a postcard. Flash foodies write very small about . . . FOOD. I write flash memoir.

For some of us sitting down to transcribe or pen a memoir can be an overwhelming task. I recommend approaching it in bite-size pieces or rather applying flash. If one simply acts upon a sudden revelation or flash of memory by writing it down then after a certain amount of time you have accumulated a portfolio of scenes. Enough of these sketches or scenes and you may be able to connect them into a memoir. By freeze framing a moment, a memory, like a camera snapshot, and dwelling there you are creating the foundation for longer memoir, a jumping off place to expand upon later.

FLASH MEMOIR: WRITING PROMPTS TO GET YOU FLASHING

Yet so many of us tend to ignore these flashes. We think *later* yet later on we might have forgotten or lost the relevance of the moment, the urgency that led us there. I recommend a process I call *Write right now* In the amount of time it takes you to brush your teeth, you can jot down the memory and an outline which can be filled in later. The nice thing about flash is that it can be unresolved. There often isn't enough space/word count to fully explore the memory. And, like so many of our memories, there is an undercurrent of lose threads, fuzzy blurred beginnings and endings with little or no significance. They simply are. We do not have to fight to form them into a 3-act script. Or, by writing about the memory, you might (possibly not all at once, but eventually) find meaning to it or a continuity of time.

What I love most about flash memoir is the inconsequential. The ordinary. Again, by freeze- framing a moment we are capturing it, holding it, and then letting it go for others. Some of the best writing resonates with us because we have a similar memory or experience. Memoir is a way of validating what we think happened and also relating to others. In many ways we all share the same human emotions that are expressed through memory. And, like Proust's madeleines, hanging laundry is not simply hanging laundry but can be an act of self-sacrifice, devotion, a symbol of great love. The essence of the ordinary, though humble, reveals an extraordinary life. One built upon sublime moments that may add up to an epic memoir. If only you begin.

The prompts in this book are designed to spur memories, to get you writing—be it fiction or non- fiction. That's right, just write it. The basis of all good fiction is rooted in autobiography. So begin with a memory and see where it leads. Later you can sort out truth from pure invention— depending on the ultimate goal of the piece. When submitting flash, I channel it through either a journal's fiction or non-fiction portal depending upon the final result. Mostly what journals want is good writing.

I'll also direct you to resources, authors to read and study, and places to submit. Ultimately you'll want to check my website as that is where I'll continually be updating, purging broken or old links, and putting up new ones. All of the flash prompts included in this eBook were harvested from my blog series: Memoirouswrite.blogspot.com/[1] where I posted a prompt every week for a year. So write right now—and enjoy!

---

1. http://memoirouswrite.blogspot.com/

Hot Flash: Centerville, Ohio

Sense of place, though not one of the infamous five senses, is nevertheless strong. Perhaps it goes back to early man, roaming the Vézère Valley of what is now Dodogne, France. Yet even these Neanderthal creatures had the wherewithal to create through art by decorating their cave walls. Maybe it's something as simple as "marking" their spot. An innate sense of mortality that tells them to leave a record—that they were once here.

We are all marked by place, it informs who we are.

I am a fan of the New York School of Poets. Not a school at all but an informal group of friends who wrote poetry and art reviews and hung out together at the Cedar Tavern in the East Village of New York City. One of the "founders" was Frank O'Hara (whose poetry exemplifies the write right now method and also captures the ordinary, more on O'Hara later!), and when he died, Joe LeSuer in his memoir of their friendship/lovership, *Digression on Some Poems by Frank O'Hara*, wrote an essay "Four Apartments[2]," built around a series of apartments he and Frank shared.

Place connects us to the land as well as to people. We write to remember and remember as we write.

Write right now

Sit down and recall all the places you've ever lived. There will likely be more than one anecdote produced from each place, record them. By brainstorming you stay in the moment. Later you can go back and fill in the blanks.

I have vague memories of falling into a ditch filled with water and my mother fishing me out. Or was it the story I heard her tell so often. "Janie fell into a culvert and one of the neighbor kids came and got me."

---

2.   http://www.amazon.com/Digressions-Some-Poems-Frank-OHara/dp/0374529043

I imagine Mom running like hell, hoping I'm still alive, only to pull me out and spank me and then hold me tight. That was when we lived on Hadley Ave. in Kettering, Ohio.

Our next house was on Princewood Avenue in unincorporated Washington Township.

Finally, we moved to a split-level house in Centerville. I lived there from middle of 3rd grade until age 21. So I had a plethora of memories from which to draw.

I wrote several remembrances and then realized I could cut them down to 50 words, whereupon I submitted them to various journals as 50-word vignettes.

<u>50-Words Stories</u>[3]

Centerville, Ohio

I was a childhood insomniac. Sometimes in the middle of the night, the quietest hour before dawn, I'd slip out of my bed and drop out the window to the spongy dew-grass— and under the wan light of the moon I'd twirl, my night dress lifting like a gypsy dancer.

---

3.   https://fiftywordstories.com/2017/01/24/jane-hertenstein-centerville-ohio/

Hot Flash: Spring is in the Air

Our six senses are the easiest pathways to memory. When reading Mary Karr's *The Art of Memoir* I felt as if she were hitting all the right notes. So many questions new memoirists struggle with are covered in her book. According to Karr, the sense of smell is one of the oldest.

"I had a friend who is a neurologist say that it's the oldest sense—the primary sense is smell. Animals can smell changes in territory. Even one-celled amoeba, who have no brainstems, can smell. So much feeling is attached to it." From an interview about the book: http://www.splendidtable.org/story/mary-karr-memory-is-what-you-can-smell-touch-and-taste

A few years back I wrote a piece called "Sense of Smell" which was included in an anthology, IMPACT: A Collection of Short Memoir, based upon small memories (flash).

The piece emerged simply from standing at a corner waiting for the light to change. Spring time. The lilacs in bloom. And BAM! That's all it took. Memories came rushing upon me.

Sense of Smell

Yesterday I was jogging past the hospital and paused, still running in place, waiting for the light to change. A waft of lilac drifted over to me.

One time in college I fasted for nine days. My intent was to rid the body of winter's impurities, cleanse my system of toxins.

After a few days of not eating, I was over being hungry. During the day I kept busy with classes, but in the evenings I was lost. Dinner was my transition time. I was used to sitting down before a plate or bowl and relaxing. I didn't know what to do with the extra time?

So to forget the emptiness inside of me I went for walks through neighborhoods. It was springtime finally after a dreary winter. The lilacs were in bloom. The fragrance was sweet, purple, reminding me of concord grapes. I stopped to inhale, my stomach ingesting itself. There was also honeysuckle in the air, which made me think of butterscotch.

I strolled past houses where I could tell someone was doing wash. Dryers vented lavender and warm roses through little pipes in the wall. It's a known fact that starving people—their senses heightened by the lack of food—have an especially acute sense of smell. The fresh smell of laundry detergent and scented fabric softener drove me into primal paroxysms. I wanted to rip open a box of Tide and pour the contents down my throat.

Trying to escape, I hurried further down the street until I was halted by the familiar odor of hamburger cooking and of onions sautéing. The intense late afternoon sun bounced bronze off the picture windows before me. My nose, fine-tuned by fasting, was able to detect the smell of fish, feathery flakes pulling away from filigree bones, smothered in melted butter, the color of custard, and garnished with parsley, more than a condiment, but an aesthetic, symbolizing rebirth, the greening of the world. I smelled bread fresh from the oven, bursting with tangy yeastiness, a soft springy sponge, steam rising, wafting, curling upward like invisible tendrils drawing me in. I swear I could smell red potatoes boiling, the zing of coarse salt, the brown scum foaming, roiling. Even the potato broth was intoxicating, possessing a bouquet, like a fine wine.

Suddenly I was transported back, the memory so real it seems three-dimensional: the five or six of us frying up boxes of batter-dipped shrimp, the crowded kitchen hazy with smoke, my t-shirt reeking of grease. I help by spreading out paper towel to soak up extra oil after Mom dumps a basket before refilling it. We eat in shifts, some of us standing, some of us sitting. Newspaper cones of steaming shrimp. My brother says sea horses are sexless, and I counter, no it's the men sea horses that have the babies.

Serves them right says my older sister. We beg our mom for pop. She buys an 8-pack every week and rations it. Me and my sister are allowed to split a bottle. She pours and I choose—that way it's fair. Dad washes his shrimp down with beer. Pabst Blue Ribbon, the condensation sweating down the sides of the can. Bobo the cat, maddened by the smell, rubs against my ankles; through my bare feet I can feel her purring.

It was only a second. I awoke, a stranger hanging around outside other people's houses. Embarrassed, I pushed on, hungrier than ever.

Then yesterday, at the corner of Clarendon and Marine Drive, I recalled that memory inside the other memory, both so far in the past as to have been buried in the margins of my mind. The light changed and yet I lingered, filled with longing.

Write right now

Using your sense of smell, call up memories and write about them. What will it take to arouse some long-sleeping memory: fry oil, lilacs, laundry detergent, cinnamon? Wake up and smell the roses.

Hot Flash: If These Walls Could Talk

A fly on the wall.

Here's the catch—this is a dialogue only challenge. Try to avoid, he said, she said. This is literally about what we might hear if the walls around us could talk.

As limiting as this may sound, one can create whole scenes using strictly dialogue. This kind of exercise is also helpful in establishing "voice"—something essential to strong narrative stories.

You might be wondering what this might have to do with memoir since—of course—walls do not talk. There are many conduits to memoir. Memoir is no longer a new genre, and many writers are exploring ways in which to present material in inventive ways in order to keep readers engaged. Dialogue already is somewhat controversial when writing memoir—as the writer cannot say for certain that they have faithfully transcribed a conversation. It will always be your rendition, or even a way you push the story forward or break up straight narrative. Frank McCourt's *Angela's Ashes* would only be half as interesting without the use of written dialogue. Frank McCourt was the consummate Irish storyteller. I can easily imagine him telling some of the same stories from *Angela's Ashes* down at the pub (or pubs, he had a few favorites).

So loosen up. What if these walls could talk?

Write right now

Devise a flash told completely in dialogue, this can either be straight memoir, fictional, or a combination thereof. If it helps, write the flash as a small scene. Feel free to include plot twists and surprise endings. If stuck here is a prompt:

A couple fighting in a car. What are they arguing about? Are they about to arrive or depart a party? Are they outside the hospital or a bank? Have they simply pulled over to answer the phone or to let an emergency vehicle by?

Hot Flash: The Sunday Newspaper

Hot Flashes aren't just for post-menopausal women, they're for everyone who wants to write around their blocks, shake off writer lethargy, and dive in. Even if the water's cold—you don't have to stay long, just get your feet wet. Just long enough to awaken your memory and write in the hot flash of the moment.

Today's Hot Flash is the Sunday newspaper.

Admittedly you have to be of a certain age to maybe comprehend the full experience of the Sunday paper, what it meant to leisurely peruse and absorb news, commentary, and varying opinions. Now, more than ever, we need the Sunday paper.

For many of us the Sunday news means a slow morning, a cup of coffee, catching up. As a child all of us kids used to fight over who got the "funnies" first. I remember sprawling in front of the Sunday paper on the living room floor, or in more recent times, skipping church to lounge with the paper scattered at my feet.

As a young teen I helped my sister deliver newspapers. Each one weighed the weight of the earth, the advertising insert alone was fifty pounds. I could maybe fit only a dozen on the bag on my bike. So together she and I could cover a neighborhood before returning to re-load. I remember early mornings, pink and golden glow burgeoning on the horizon. In the winter I'd often come upon tracks in the snow left by dancing rabbits. On a certain Christmas morning I paused while crossing a lawn and there in the picture window I saw a man and woman embrace. They were all alone, there by the tree. Perhaps they'd been up all night wrapping up presents or putting the finishing touches on the tree. Or maybe they were up early to put a turkey or ham or roast in the oven. I continued with the papers, but even now more than 40 Christmases later I can still recall this homey scene.

Write right now

What does the Sunday newspaper mean to you?

JANE HERTENSTEIN

Hot Flash: Writing the Headlines

The newspaper is full of real stories that at some point might alter or connect with our own story. Think tsunami, school closing, threat of e. coli in lettuce. Maybe not right away, but in a year flotsam will hit our western shores, the price of a BLT will go up, and the nice lady down the street will lose her job at the elementary school. A lot of what occurs in our life might fall under the header of observation, without conclusion or closure. Walt Disney was right: It's a small world after all.

Ernest (the auto-correct keeps wanting to change it to earnest!) Hemingway had background in journalism. *In Our Time* contains small vignettes between longer stories such as "Big Two-Hearted River." I'm not sure what he meant by doing this. Perhaps they were palate cleansers, you know like eating cheese or grapes between courses. As a foreign correspondent, he would eventually report on the Greco-Turkish population exchange, the Spanish Civil War, and, was embedded with the 22nd Infantry Regiment during World War II. He was present at D-Day and for the liberation of Paris. Quite a few of the inter-chapter pieces were vignettes of his war experiences written in the journalistic-style without bias, comment, or the slightest hint of hindsight. Much like Frank O'Hara did twenty-five years later, he composed flash from what he simply observed. (*See* "Lana Turner has collapsed" by Frank[4] O'Hara)[5]

---

4.   https://www.poets.org/poetsorg/poem/poem-lana-turner-has-collapsed

5.   https://www.poets.org/poetsorg/poem/poem-lana-turner-has-collapsed

Write right now

What's in the news? Using a headline as a prompt, write a flash. This can be strictly memoir or you can take any headline and place yourself there as a reporter and write fictionally what you see. Or, perhaps, a headline such as School Closures, affects you—write your flash as an opinion (op-ed) piece. An artist after 9/11 created a word collage based upon the weather report for that day memorable blue-sky day.

Hot Flash: Where Do Ideas Come From?

Where do ideas come from?

Lately I've been using the Internet to harvest visual prompts. A picture is said to be worth a thousand words. Well, sometimes we only need 500 or even less. We can easily construe a paragraph surrounding an image we come across. The following are some places I go to for images that inspire flash.

<u>Just Breathe</u>[6]

Here is a way to travel without ever leaving your chair—and possibly feel really good about yourself. Just Breathe is a group site on Facebook. Not sure exactly who is behind it, but it comes together much like the proverb "It takes a village." The photos are not hers. They are sourced from contributors and possibly—guess who?—the World Wide Web. The moderator/creator has gone to the trouble to collect, curate, and archive under different headings thousands of images which she posts throughout a 24-hour day. For example—I have no favorites because I love them ALL:

(from Just Breathe website)

---

6.   https://www.facebook.com/Just-Breathe-470854759626488/

I also get notifications from Tiny House. This is small simple living like tear-drop trailer size or shipping container if you want to go larger. It is all about living small and not impacting the earth with your huge house footprint. It is about simplifying in order to smell the roses, the snow, or hear the grass growing. The ideas put forth inspire me. Here are a few:

(from The Tiny House website)

<u>Puuung</u>[7]

Is about more than cute lovey-dovey pictures—though initially that is what drew me to the site and to sign up for notifications. Who can resist such simple displays of attention and love? They feed my soul.

The artist is from South Korea and is a young woman. Her interest or process stems from architecture. She browses an architecture library and from interior designs "grows" a picture of a happy couple. How many of us have ever passed by a window and accidentally looked in upon an intimate scene of family. Anyway, Puuung enters these houses, these rooms and brings us simple acts of intimacy.

(from Puuung website)

Write right now

Visit these sites and write. Create your own flash moment from inside. Escape

---

7. https://www.facebook.com/puuung1/

Hot Flash: Google and Go

The important thing is: getting started.

There are times when all we need is one-word to get the juices flowing. But there is another way to let go and enter in—ever hear the phrase: a face that launched a thousand ships or a picture is worth a thousand words?

I sit and meditate. What is this feeling that I'm feeling, what is it I'm after, where is it? Ethereal abstracts. Have you ever googled these same questions? In that tiny Google space, that is actually infinite, I've typed in stuff such as "I thought I saw you through the rain" or "the happiness that is just beyond me"—just to see what pops up in images. It's interesting what Google gives you. Sometimes it allows me to see more concretely the intangible or a possibility.

The very idea that my device can sense my needs, is somewhat disturbing and at the same time comforting. Especially on melancholy days where the clouds touch the earth. I can't see further than the darkness, but there is, out there, around the corner, something. So yesterday I uploaded 2 new profile/cover pics to Facebook that helped solidify my aspirations. I could easily write 50 new words about these images.

JANE HERTENSTEIN

(from Just Breath website.)

Write right now

Google and go.

Hot Flash: Ghost Houses

Abandoned houses awaken something in all of us. Could it be mortality? There is something melancholic about these old buildings/houses. A faded grandeur, a real sense of loss.

Some people have made a hobby of exploring abandoned warehouses and industrial sites.

Remember as a kid coming upon some ruin and wondering what used to be. In the woods near my house were several dilapidated farmhouses—abandoned since a proposed bypass 675 was soon to be constructed. The houses were all scheduled for demolition. Unless, of course, they just collapsed all by their self.

I can still recall the strips of ancient peeling wallpaper, roses faded into the weathered and aged paper, until the image is barely visible. A soiled mattress in the corner, stinking of urine and mouse infestation. The wind-swept corners piled with litter, remains, the midden* of life left behind—a forgotten doll; a cheap plastic toy; a chipped tea cup; a dress wet, now dried, a stiff mound not resembling anything.

*From Wikipedia: "A midden is an old dump for domestic waste which may consist of animal bone, human excrement, botanical material, vermin, shells, sherds, and other artifacts, word used by archaeologists to describe waste products relating to day-to-day human life."

Robert Frost wrote about a "Ghost House" . . .

I dwell in a lonely house I know

That vanished many a summer ago,

And left no trace but the cellar walls,

And a cellar in which the daylight falls

And the purple-stemmed wild raspberries grow.

....

I dwell with a strangely aching heart

In that vanished abode there far apart

On that disused and forgotten road
That has no dust-bath now for the toad.
Night comes; the black bats tumble and dart;

The feeling that spaces once inhabited, once alive but now empty or hollow or ruined come to fill us. There is something compelling about a ruin that calls us to come explore.

To this day I can detail the places I've stumbled upon, vacated, and the stuff left behind. Some of these images impressed themselves into my writing.

Originally published in *Flashquake*:

Young and Dumb

She ran away when she was seventeen. Hooked up with a guy on the bus and together they rode to Denver. But he turned out to be trouble. One night she slipped away from the room they rented. By the neon strobe she packed a bag, took his wallet while he slept. On the way out of town she stopped at a diner with a funky name and ordered a chicken dinner. Ate it to the bone.

FLASH MEMOIR: WRITING PROMPTS TO GET YOU FLASHING

It was a bad space. She couldn't go home. Let's leave it at that. And she didn't have anywhere else to go, except names on a map. She preferred the blue roads, the ones that branched off, growing more and more anonymous, changing names in different locales, adapting to the terrain. Often dead-ending.

She was okay on her own. She knew enough to get by. Her step brothers had taught her karate. Really more like Three Stooges gestures. She knew how to scream. Enough to do damage to her vocal cords, until her stomach muscles ached. Until black night melted and she moved on. Her few possessions tied to her back.

She carried in her pocket stray bits. A bottle cap. A white cockleshell. A key. To what door she did not know. A piece of paper with a phone number on it that accidentally blew away from her. It skidded across the road and whooshed up an embankment, airborne over a barbed wire fence, and landed in a field of stubble and stick grass. She cut across that snowy field to a farmhouse. Long abandoned.

The front door was open. So she closed it. A grease-yellowed curtain lightly exhaled, the window sash unlatched. Trash, swirled into corners, occupied the first room. Loose wallpaper sagged, water stained. In the back on the first floor was a kitchen. A mouse scurried from the back of the stove to a crack in the floorboard. She righted an overturned chair. The silence scared her.

A flurry of thoughts flooded her brain, most of them connected to late-night horror movies watched on TV.

There was a staircase in the middle of the house, dividing it in two. She gripped a rail and ascended one step at a time. Listening for monsters. Creaks and audible breath. The whoosh of bat wings. Upstairs she found more of the same. Remnants. An old Sears catalogue. A pile of rags, once clothes. Animal droppings. A tin plate covered a hole back when there used to be gaslight. She picked up a child's toy, a bobble head plastic boy. The wire to his head a weak neck.

Who were they, the former occupants? What moved them on? Had the family disintegrated, broken by divorce, violence, stupid mistakes? There were all sorts of reasons. She tried to draw from the clues left behind some kind of explanation. She reckoned they were young and dumb.

She never meant to stay. It rained the next day, and the day after that. A solid week of damn miserable rain. She lit a fire in the fireplace, expecting any minute for a neighbor to come check the place out, for a cop to pull into the puddle-rutted drive. Instead it was as if she'd fallen off the face of the earth. She learned to keep her own company, separate the voices inside her head. The good ones from the bad and make up her own mind. In town she bought groceries and hauled them back to the farm. Simple fare, easy enough to cook over the fire or eat raw. She licked her fingers and wiped them on her jeans. Slowly a sense of well-being came over her. The kind that comes with a full tummy, warmth, and forgetfulness, where the crazy windmill inside her finally slowed down.

* * *

Years later while slicing tomatoes, she will look up. Her memory ignited by who knows what. Another kitchen, another house, she remembers. Through the window the back yard with the kids' swing set is aglow with late afternoon light. And putting down the knife, she breathes a prayer.

Write right now

Right now, write about a ruin in your own life.

Hot Flash: Family Photo Album

After my parents passed us kids began to go through things. I was impressed by the amount of work necessary to clear away my parent's stuff and the legacy they left behind. In the midst of sorting we came upon a cache of old photos. Snapshots glued into a scrapbook, a shoebox of random vacation shots, an envelope of unmarked pictures—people impossible to identify, everyone long dead.

I held onto them for a few years hoping to share them digitally, but the process of scanning them in one-by-one was daunting and time-consuming. There are companies that will do this for you. Old photographs as well as home movies and videotapes. So after comparing prices and reliability—I wasn't about to send off a treasure trove to have it lost in the mail—I bagged and sent them out into the universe. A week later they were returned, along with a CD.

What took me awhile though was actually sitting down with the pictures—there were so many, black and white, scalloped-edged, brittle. They became like a flipbook of the past. I dwelled in memories and lingered, daydreaming in nostalgia.

I wondered what it must have been like for my parents: surviving the Great Depression, World War II, through the GI Bill attending college—something they never once would have considered without government help. Mom and Dad met at Ohio State and went to fraternity dances—Mom in fabulous gowns. They were so young and beautiful and crazy.

How many times has an old photo opened up doors you never even knew about?

Write right now

Flash a family story based upon a photo. It might be sweet or bitter, humorous or reflective. Full of brightness or tragedy. Go to your cloud or physical albums

Hot Flash: This is Water

Commencement speeches—we all know these kinds of speeches can be extremely cheesy. Or if not cheesy then extremely boring. And if not extremely boring, then drudgery, the thing you need to sit through in order to get to the next thing. Life. Debt. A job? Your future. Out to eat with family, friends, your girlfriend/boyfriend/the person you are about to split from. The promised road trip, European vacation, summer of freedom. Grad school.

While trying to put off writing I fiddled on Facebook and turned up David Foster Wallace's timeless commencement address, "This Is Water."

The subtitle of the essay is "About Living a Compassionate Life." What struck me about the essay was that water is a stand-in for life. The ho-hum, the thing one can easily overlook, dismiss, become so used to that it is taken for granted. Just like water is for a fish—yet so essential. Ordinary life is just that—life. The stuff we swim around in until it is pointed out to us that we are indeed swimming, indeed living.

We all need to take time, take stock, smell the roses, hear the birds sing, help an old lady with her groceries out to the car, hold the door for someone, mail your favorite charity a dollar or two. We all get caught up in the routine that we lose track—just like those fishes in his opening story: What the hell is water? So often we forget what makes up the bones, the blood, the very humanness of life.

Write right now

Write an ode to the ordinary—what is your water? What is it that you need to pay attention to? Right now, commence.

Hot Flash: Animal Memoirs

One day, again trying to avoid a deadline, I wondered if animals are sentimental, long for the good ole days, wax nostalgic. How much do animals remember?

From *National Geographic*[8]:

Dogs forget an event within two minutes. Chimpanzees, at around 20 seconds, are worse than rats at remembering things, while the memory spans of three other primates—baboons, pig-tailed macaques, and squirrel monkeys—exceeded only bees . . .

Exercises with captive animals revealed that while some had great long-term memory they flunked at the short-term and vice versa.

Elephants are known for having remarkable memories. From Cracked.com[9]:

"Whenever they encounter the scent of another elephant's urine, an elephant can record in its computerish brain the location and direction of the pisser. This enables them to devote a sizable portion of their working memory to maintaining these expansive mental maps."

Now if only my husband could pay that much attention . . . .

But the winner was a real bird brain. A small bird with the name Clark's nutcracker. This unassuming little bird is able to remember the exact location of up to 30,000 pine nuts.

Write right now

For today's Hot Flash write about the cat that came back, the dog with the incredible journey, the homing pigeon that carried a vital message which helped win the war.

---

8.   *http://news.nationalgeographic.com/2015/02/150225-dogs-memories-animals-chimpanzees-science-mind-psychology/*

9.   http://www.cracked.com/article_19535_6-animals-with-better-memories-than-you.html

FLASH MEMOIR: WRITING PROMPTS TO GET YOU FLASHING

I know you have an animal story. Nabokov's life story was full of butterflies. Here is a website devoted to animal memoirs[10]. Go!

---

10.   http://www.trendtablet.com/12658-animal-memoirs/

Hot Flash: More Picture Prompts

I wrote earlier about using images to generate flash, pictures that inspire memories. I often use picture to spark my creative juices. Here are a few other websites/blogs that I go to:

Forgotten Chicago[11] is truly a Facebook community. There is nothing like throwing up an old pic of Chicago to arouse comments and an outpouring of memories. Just the other day a pic of the old Morrie Mages sports store was posted and even I waxed nostalgic—8 floors of sporting goods! (One whole floor was dedicated alone to golfing equipment.) Eventually Morrie sold out to Sportmart which became Sports Authority—a subpar store compared to Morrie Mages.

From the amazing Internet[12]:

"I'm not tired. I'm not that old. I'm aggressive and alive, and I love this business," said the 71- year-old Mages. "But in order to get bigger, you got to have more money behind you, and I ain't got it."

Morrie Mages started his career on Maxwell Street, the city's Old World-style bazaar on the Near South Side, hawking bargains from a pushcart in front of his Russian immigrant father`s sporting goods store. Later he would become a partner in the business with his father and brother in 1938.

There is also Calumet 412[13], and Uptown Chicago History[14] offering photos to riff on.

Miller's Silver Palm Burlesk Revue, 1117 W Wilson Ave, 1951, Chicago. Here is a sample post under comments:[15]

---

11.   https://www.facebook.com/groups/forgottenchicago/

12.   http://articles.chicagotribune.com/1987-06-17/business/8702140873_1_stores-mc-sporting-goods-chicago-area

13.   http://calumet412.com/

14.   https://www.facebook.com/Uptown-Chicago-History-144573472241285/

15.   http://uptownhistory.compassrose.org/2010/12/readers-memories-of-silver-palm.html

FLASH MEMOIR: WRITING PROMPTS TO GET YOU FLASHING

Bill Matteson wrote about the SILVER PALM BURLESQUE BAR

Well it was about 1948 on a Saturday afternoon, I was 12 years old, me and my buddy Jimmy Thomas were going to the DeLuxe Theatre at the corner of Wilson Ave. and Clifton which was just west of the El tracks. (The Deluxe Theater was razed and is now part of the Truman Campus.) Jimmy and I stopped in front of the Silver Palm to sneak a peek, see something worthwhile for a 12 year-old boy. We weren't really that interested in *Abbot and Costello meet Captain Kidd* any way.

Three big black sedans pulled up, men jumped out of the cars carrying sledge hammers and axes. They smashed through the locked front door. Jimmy and I, being boys followed right in after them. We stood on the side and watched them smash tables, bottles, the bar and even the walls. On the walls were pictures of nude women; we were in our glory. The smasher guys told us if we stayed out of the way we could have anything we wanted. We stole an old wagon from back outside the bar; we took all the pictures. Behind the bar were some small cartons containing little plastic telescopes on a key chain, inside the scopes were women nude from the waist up. Other boxes contained "8 pagers". An 8 pager was exactly that, page 1 was the cover then 7 other pages of hand-drawn sex acts.

The outcome was me and Jimmy took the wagon back to the Pretzel Benders Inn on Leland Ave. just west of Kenmore and sold everything we had to a few of the "boys." We made about $10 each. $10 was a huge amount of money; it cost 12 cents to get into the movies.

Who were those guys in the black sedans? I never found out; it never made the newspaper. The speculation in the neighborhood was the "mob" or the IRS or "Big 10." Big 10 was an unmarked squad car with three detectives and nobody ever messed with Big 10.

This is a terrific story—all from a vintage pic!

(photo   from   Calumet   412)

Another Facebook group I've discovered is Pictures of Chicago[16]. Just everyday stuff. Crowds at the beach. Michigan Avenue. A hot dog stand. This is the ESSENCE of flash. An Instagram moment that is here now and a minute late gone. And, if you, me, *we* don't grab it then it will forever be a regret. Because the light changes, the clouds, move, or something else comes along and that moment is lost.

Write right now

Sadly, because times change, many of the things that seem cemented into the now will one day disappear. Just like how my town, Centerville in Ohio, used to have a yearly fundraiser called the Ox Roast. I looked forward to it every year—the last time I checked I discovered Centerville no longer does the Ox Roast. Gone are the sketchy carnival rides and loopy games where I'd win a goldfish in a glass bowl that lived approximately a week before becoming a floater.

Does your town or region have a historical society website or Facebook page? Often our memories get stirred up when others begin to reminisce—maybe join a group at the library or sit down and ask a village elder stories of "back when." Write a flash based upon local lore or a memory you have from the past, the way things used to be.

---

16.   https://www.facebook.com/groups/640802762686570/?fref=nf

JANE HERTENSTEIN

Hot Flash: Go on Vacation

As a kid my family went two or three times to a "horse farm" in Kentucky. Well, not really a horse farm, but a farm that had horses. Hidden Valley. I've tried to Google it a couple of times, but nothing comes up. Hard to believe there is no cyber footprint.

I still remember the sweatshirt my sister and I had from the "ranch." A ranch of sorts. I seem to remember a concrete stables. I'm not sure what we did at the "resort." There might have been a volleyball pitch and a playground with rusty playground equipment. The highlight was a guided horse ride. We were placed on sleepy doddering horses that probably dropped dead of old age soon after the ride. In the heat of a Kentucky afternoon we'd ride dusty trails with flies wasping around us. Later we'd take a dip in the bathtub-size pool.

It was a family-run operation.

We probably had a kitchenette in our room in order to save money on meals. That's how my family ran things. On a shoestring.

Later we'd trade up for vacations at Myrtle Beach S.C. and after that my parents (without kids) would travel out West, eventually doing a package trip to Europe, the kind where a group pulls in on a motor coach, snaps pictures, before re-boarding and going on to the next site. They loved it!

It's hard to believe I can't even re-visit the ranch on the Internet. I guess I'll have to rely upon memory. Images of rust and dust and horses long gone.

We also used to go to an old motor court called Wild Waves on the shores of Lake Erie—every summer there was a spectacular fish die-off as the lake was under a great deal of pollution stress in the 1970s. The old log cabins harbored spiders in the wood, the walls crawled with them. The cement dock was crumbling; every winter eroded another chunk of it. The metal Adirondack chairs were one color: rust red, with hints of a former pastel palette shining through. Yet, in my mind, I travel there all the time, checking images on the Internet to confirm that part of my past. A past that was *past* even back then.

As kids you think this is all there is, and then there comes a time, when you stop going on family vacations. The kids are getting older, far too busy in the summers, it's impossible for everyone to get together—even for a week. What used to be becomes a mere memory.

For a while my husband and I were caretakers of a small trailer on a piece of land in down-state Illinois. We used to love sitting outside after dinner while darkness fell and listen to the coyotes get fired up. Far off we'd hear a howl or a train whistle blow. But, then it became hard to keep up with the place. Too many repairs, taxes, job changes, etc. We finally gave up the place.

What about that one rental, that time-share? We all have stories of nightmare destinations, of ants or lizards trekking up and down the walls, of hopeless plumbing, of descriptions that don't match up to reality, of fighting to get deposits back, of making do. Or of paradise. The best spot ever—if only you could go back there again!

Write right now

What is your retreat place? Your vacation spot? That place of surrender? Where you can be your truest self? Most relaxed.

Is it somewhere your parents took you every year as a child? Or did you visit your family's fish camp or Granny's house in the country?

Are your neurons fired up, quick—go!

JANE HERTENSTEIN

Hot Flash: Postcards

Souvenirs. Postcards. Today these words almost seem quaint. My husband and I once, when traveling, told our host in Slovenia that we would send him a postcard from our next destination.

He seemed puzzled. You mean like an auntie or my grandmother?

I guess it did seem rather old-fashioned—especially since we could easily send an email or upload a picture from our phone. Or any number of things. Our next destination was Montenegro then Albania. How does one even ask for a stamp in Albanian? How reliable is postal service?

Postcards in the US have been known to take decades. Mail sent from the front during World War II is still getting delivered.

I love postcards. I buy them and send them and appreciate getting them in the mail. I save them and tape them to the walls of my office or upon the door to the room we have reserved for couchsurfers.

Going through my parents' old photos I stumbled upon old postcards. It seems postcard writing runs in the family. I have postcards written by my mother to my grandmother and aunts "back home." In one she mentions that she is going to a New Year's Eve party in New York City and that she hasn't gotten into any trouble yet. She has written slantwise on the blank side of the card in order to save space.

In addition there are two sets of postcards from Rome, bought but never mailed. One dates from around the 1980s when my parents visited on a post-retirement adventure and the other set is from 1944 when the Allies were working their way up the boot.

The word souvenir is French for remember.

While traveling I like to pick up little things: a pebble, a pinecone, a seashell to bring home. I have a small shelf where I keep these mementos. I also buy things to bring to friends to let them know I was thinking of them while gone. That even though I was having a great time, they were never far from my thoughts.

Souvenir is from the Latin *subvenire* 'occur to the mind.'

Memories are souvenirs of the mind. Keep and cherish them. Place them on the shelf of a journal or diary so that later you can revisit them.

It is on snowy days such as these that I gaze upon my cheapy Walgreens snow globe I bought in Key West—a margarita floating in a sea of glitter—and relish those warm tropical days of birds chattering in the top of palm trees and warm gulf waters washing the shores.

Write right now

Some journals refer to flash as postcard writing. As in send us a postcard! A story written in as much space as a postcard allows.

Take an old postcard and send out a message

Hot Flash: William Wordsworth and the Ordinary

While in the Lake District I stopped at Dove Cottage, Wordsworth's residence for eight years, before marriage and then through 3 of his 5 children. He also seemed to have eternal houseguests, a sister and Samuel Taylor Coleridge.

Before moving to Dove Cottage Wordsworth had been somewhat itinerate, what we might call a tramp. He moved around a lot, carrying only a small bag. He wrote much of his poetry while on the go; he especially loved to compose on long walks. While living at Dove Cottage he wrote some of his most beloved poems.

He wasn't always so well-read, so well-loved. (It was only later in life and after much coaxing that he agreed to be Poet Laureate for a short spell.) In fact Byron and Shelley were much more popular than Wordsworth because much of their verse was considered "exotic," based in foreign lands, out of the ordinary. Thus, Wordsworth's writings were considered local, homely, of little consequence because his topics dealt with the everyday, with people we know well and scenes of the English countryside.

I wandered lonely as a cloud
That floats on high o'er vales and hills, When all at once I saw a crowd,
A host, of golden daffodils; Beside the lake, beneath the trees,
Fluttering and dancing in the breeze.
Or . . .
Lines Composed a Few Miles above Tintern Abbey, On Revisiting the Banks of the Wye during a Tour. July 13, 1798
Five years have past; five summers, with the length Of five long winters! and again I hear
These waters, rolling from their mountain-springs With a soft inland murmur.

Or . . .

Composed upon Westminster Bridge, September 3, 1802

Earth has not anything to show more fair: Dull would he be of soul who could pass by A sight so touching in its majesty:

This City now doth, like a garment, wear The beauty of the morning; silent, bare,

Ships, towers, domes, theatres, and temples lie Open unto the fields, and to the sky;

All bright and glittering in the smokeless air.

He is writing what he sees, what he's experiencing. He is in the NOW. And because of this propensity to record everyday life, he now surpasses Byron and Shelley in popularity. People turn to Wordsworth to re-capture the mood of the time, pastoral England. He also was someone who could encapsulate the sublime, that is create with a few words a feeling that one can't quite put their finger on. Beauty! Peace! Well being! That all is right.

Wordsworth translated his world into words

Write right now

Right now go outside and, plein air, compose. Take a walk along the lakefront, or along the bicycle path, or into your garden—now subsided into mid-autumn. Go to the Friday night football game, or take a Sunday drive out into the country. Go outside and write, give me a sense of where you are and how it feels to be alive.

Hot Flash: Coleridge and Conversational Poetry

Samuel Taylor Coleridge lived to age 61 in a time when this was considered a ripe old age, yet his entire life he was plagued with health problems. Namely mental illness. At the time bi-polar wasn't a thing, yet Coleridge had all the symptoms. A bout with rheumatic fever in childhood eventually led to a dependence upon opium (laudanum) and alcohol.

Dove Cottage, William Wordsworth's residence in the Lake District, Grasmere, brought me back into the orbit of Samuel Taylor Coleridge, as he was a perpetual houseguest of Wordsworth for 8 years. I learned while touring the cottage that Coleridge was pretty unstable, the guide made mention that often Coleridge would cry out in his sleep. Scream, shout, holler. The bedrooms were like little boxes, right next to each other. There wasn't a lot of room to accommodate someone with night terrors. This must have impacted the entire household. Yet, he was apparently welcomed.

Though a creative genius, throughout his life he was afflicted with delusions, fits, hallucinations—haunted, it seems. He couldn't stay married, but sought community. He needed people. Wordsworth, from what I can surmise, must have been a faithful friend. Together they ushered in the romantic age and formed what came to be known as the Lake Poets.

From Wikipedia:[17] "In 1802, Coleridge took a nine-day walking holiday in the fells of the Lake District. Coleridge is credited with the first recorded descent of Scafell to Mickledore via Broad Stand, although this was more due to his getting lost than a keenness for mountaineering."

I was in this area and let me say, it is remote, steep and lonesome. I can imagine getting lost.

17.   https://en.wikipedia.org/wiki/Samuel_Taylor_Coleridge

Coleridge wrote eight conversational poems. Blank verse, natural seeming prose. This term was coined much, much later. What Coleridge was doing was new, different. From Wikipedia[18]: In 1965, M. H. Abrams wrote a broad description that applies to the Conversation poems: "The speaker begins with a description of the landscape; an aspect or change of aspect in the landscape evokes a varied by integral process of memory, thought, anticipation, and feeling which remains closely intervolved with the outer scene. In the course of this meditation the lyric speaker achieves an insight, faces up to a tragic loss, comes to a moral decision, or resolves an emotional problem. Often the poem rounds itself to end where it began, at the outer scene, but with an altered mood and deepened understanding which is the result of the intervening meditation."

Write right now

Try composing a conversational poem or flash. 1) Begin with setting, describe the room you're in, what's out the window, or, if outdoors, your surroundings. 2) a meditation or reflection, what memory does this evoke, what are you feeling? 3) Is there some resolution, an epiphany, an insight that can be gained? 4) Quickly finish, by bringing the reader back to the present, a reference to your surroundings such as a truck backfiring, the barista calling out your coffee order, the teacher tapping you on the shoulder, a car behind you honking.

---

18.   https://en.wikipedia.org/wiki/Samuel_Taylor_Coleridge#Conversation_poems

JANE HERTENSTEIN

Hot Flash: Weather of Six Mornings

I have a lot of poetry books on my shelf. Sometimes even just the titles are inspiring. For today's Hot Flash I want to highlight one of these titles.

The Weather of Six Mornings by Jane Cooper.

The book contains some of her earliest poems, those referencing a love killed during WWII. Her life continued hesitatingly. College, career, teaching, publishing. It seems she grieved for the better part of her life. A few other poems have to do with her childhood home in Jacksonville, Florida. I especially like the one about St. John's River and the water birds. My mind drifts back to my first solo bike trip, Jacksonville to Key West, and an foreign feeling comes over me.

Pelicans and bursting sunsets, warm sand and foaming ocean. It was another world—in January! You might wonder: Why does she refer to poetry so much?

To answer that question—flash is sometimes called the haiku of prose. With very few words one must be able to tell a story, I've always been amazed at how poetry, those compact lines, sparse words juxtaposed next to each other, evoke such depth of feeling, can transport me. Flash is capable of the same thing.

Let's borrow that title *Weather of Six Morning* and create an exercise where over the span of six consecutive mornings you write. From the title poem: "The Weather of Six Mornings"

Sunlight lies along my table like abandoned pages.
I try to speak
of what is so hard for me
—this clutter of a life— Puritanical signature!
In the prolonged hear, insects, pine needles, birch leaves
make a ground bass of silence That never quite dies.

The Weather of Six Mornings, Jane Cooper, MacMillan Company, 1957. Each section of the six "mornings" is composed of 10 lines, coupled.

Write right now

What it's like, right now. What do you see outside your window? Is it snowing, raining, is the sun pouring in? Write.

Hot Flash: Poems from Italy

Earlier I wrote about poetry books sitting on my shelf, and how the titles themselves lend inspiration. I have a book titled *Poems from Italy* by R. H. Bowden.

From what I can find online he was something of a literary dabbler. He wrote plays, poetry, fiction as well as nonfiction. He and his wife often traveled and loved to vacation in Italy where they often walked the hills of Tuscany and Umbria. He has one poem, "In the Umbrian Mountains Above Gubbio" an area I have also explored. Another poem is "To Italy at Fifty." These poems are basically travel notes, the kind of thing all of us (or at least think about) jotting down. In the midst of a journey, when we are looking with fresh eyes, we are keen to make comparisons, contrasts—observations.

Just like how we take pictures. We photograph something and think, Later I'll get prints made. Yet they stay on our phone, in the cloud without us ever acting upon them.

Write right now

Go somewhere you've never been before. Walk the streets of another neighborhood take Metra to the suburbs. Take pen and paper, a notebook with you and write a paragraph, sketches of the scenery, who you are with, the color of the sky, how it feels to be away

Hot Flash: Precarious Times

I don't think there has ever been any point in history where someone hasn't thought: We live in precarious times. In fact, right now, I'd say we live in precarious times.

Stephen Spender wrote all during the Blitz, when Germany conducted nightly raids on London and the southern coast of England. Here is just the beginning of one of his poems.

"An Air Raid Across the Bay at Plymouth"
Above the whispering sea
And waiting rocks of black coast,
Across the bay, the serchlight beams
Swing and swing back across the sky.

Their ends fuse in a cone of light
    Held for a bright instant up
    Until they break away again
    Smashing that image like a cup
Collected Poems 1928 – 1985, Stephen Spender
We are witnesses, testaments to time. We are right now at a certain crux in history and can record our thoughts, fears, frustrations.

JANE HERTENSTEIN

Write right now

What does it feels like to be you, in this moment, this turbulent time. Here is another, "Thoughts during an Air Raid"
Tells us what it is like to live through a troubled
Unstable time. When the world seems about to shake itself To death.
Be brave. Write.

Hot Flash: Leonard Cohen's Writing Process

Leonard Cohen has died.

Outside of Bob Dylan I cannot name another more prolific songwriter/poet. He was someone who embodied my mantra of Write right now I don't think he ever passed up an opportunity to chronicle a moment, experience, or a relationship, turn it into words, something to be sung.

Cohen's writing process, as he told an interviewer in 1998, was "like a bear stumbling into a beehive or a honey cache: I'm stumbling right into it and getting stuck, and it's delicious and it's horrible and I'm in it and it's not very graceful and it's very awkward and it's very painful and yet there's something inevitable about it."

A perfect description of what it's like to write for any writer. I wished I'd had this quote when working on my eBook, *365 Affirmations for the Writer*[19].

I'm posting stanzas from "Democracy" by Leonard Cohen, written after the fall of the Berlin Wall

It's coming through a hole in the air

From those nights in Tiananmen Square

It's coming from the feel

That it ain't exactly real

Or it's real, but it ain't exactly there

From the wars against disorder

From the sirens night and day

From the fires of the homeless

From the ashes of the gay

Democracy is coming to the u.s.a

---

19.   *https://www.amazon.com/365-Affirmations-Writer-Jane-Hertenstein-ebook/dp/*

B00Q5KBNNC/ref%3Dasap_bc?ie=UTF8

Cohen was famous for grabbing a phrase here and a phrase there and putting the two side by side, juxtapositioning words and images seemingly incongruent. The sense coming evident the longer you listen, dwell with the piece.

Write right now

Why not sit down and *have fun*. Experiment with words, word order, sense. Start in one direction and suddenly shift gears. Here are some examples I constructed:

Archaeology

Arches arched Arc è ark

Archduke archetype I ache.

Artic A Go-Go

watch sea levels rise s

wamp the coastlands birds, bears,

bye bye

A woman lies on top of the bed fully dressed, a clock on the wall ticks. She wants to know why she is crying.

Across the industrial wasteland comes the gnashing of gears, the gnawing of metal bone. All nature cries out.

Look up, look up at the sky! Hear, hear angel voices!

I want to tear my eyes out and plug my ears.

One day I lost my joy, It ran right out of me

And in its place came woe and rue.

I was lost, I was blind, but

Now I sea.

Right now, try.

Writing: A Set-up for Failure

Remember the old days? Before the Internet—I used to read physical books. Now, of course, you can find it all on-line. I just watched a video this morning of Ta-Nehisi Coates talking about his writing process. He said writing is about failure.

Pretty much failure after failure, like one word after another. You write one crappy thing and then come back and fix it and then see other things that have to be fixed. Like a Whack-a-Mole. Writing is basically getting started and then changing it and seeing where you need research, where you need to pull it together. Relax and make mistakes.

I write about this in Freeze Frame[20] and <u>365 Affirmations for the Writer</u>.[21] Montaigne, the great 16th-century writer, called his style of writing "essay," meaning attempts. He wove together philosophy and the ordinary.

Here are just a few of the MANY topics he chose to write about:
"That We Laugh and Cry for the Same Thing" "Of Solitude"
"A Consideration Upon Cicero"
"Relish for Good and Evil Depends Upon Our Opinion" "Not to Communicate a Man's Honor"
"Of the Inequality Amongst Us" "Of Sleep"
"Of Names"
"Of the Uncertainty of Our Judgment"

---

20.   https://www.amazon.com/Freeze-Frame-Write-Memoir-ebook/dp/B00CRM2T80/

ref%3Dsr_1_2?ie=UTF8&qid=1368563871&sr=8-2&keywords=hertenstein%2C%2Bjaneze-

Frame-Write-Memoir-ebook/dp/B00CRM2T80/

ref%3Dsr_1_2%3Fie%3DUTF8&qid=1368563871&sr=8-

2&keywords=hertenstein%2C%2Bjane

21.   https://www.amazon.com/365-Affirmations-Writer-Jane-Hertenstein-ebook/dp/

B00Q5KBNNC/ref%3Dasap_bc?ie=UTF8

Of the New World of Warcraft—I made this one up, but you get the point. Mundane. Everyday. What you live and breathe and think about over toast in the morning. Maybe a meme off Facebook.

Write right now

Listen, you don't have anything to prove. Just try to write that memory from your point of view; you don't have to have all the answers or photographic recall. It's about reflection, revealing one facet and leaving the rest for some other time. How the new hat felt, the way your sister made you always pull the sled, that first Easter after Mom's cancer treatments that were only meant to prolong her life 3 - 4 months, moonlight on the back patio, your first bite of key lime pie, meeting the love of your life for the very first time—and perhaps letting them go.

Try. Then try some more. Attempt. What happened this day a year ago, five years ago, ten years past?

Hot Flash: Just Observe

I've written about Montaigne, a winemaker nobleman from Bordeaux. He was what might be considered a blogger. He wrote the personal essay at the same time coining the word "essay." Perhaps he was able to do this because he led a life of privilege with little to no other duties to distract him. During the day he'd slip off to the attic studio of his chateau and compose philosophical insights along with historical anecdotes and daily observations. It was a new literary form—from his own unique perspective.

Another keen observer was the poet James Schuyler who sat down one morning while visiting his friends Jane and Joe Hazan at their home in Water Mill, Long Island.

Here are a few excerpts from: "June 30, 1974"[22]

for Jane and Joe Hazan[23]

Let me tell you
that this weekend
Sunday morning in the country
fills my soul
with tranquil joy:
the dunes beyond
the pond beyond
the humps of bayberry –

***

No other houses, except
   this charming one,

---

22.   https://newyorkschoolpoets.wordpress.com/2016/06/30/james-schuylers-june-30-1974-and-the-poetics-of-everyday-life/

23.   _https://newyorkschoolpoets.wordpress.com/2016/06/30/james-schuylers-june-30-1974-and-the-poetics-of-everyday-life/_

alive with paintings,
plants and quiet.
I haven't said
a word. I like
to be alone
with friends. To get up
to this morning view
and eat poached eggs
and extra toast with
Tiptree Gooseberry Preserve
(green) -and coffee,

***

I'd like to go out
for a swim but
it's a little cool
for that. Enough to
sit here drinking coffee,
writing, watching the clear
day ripen (such
a rainy June we had)
while Jane and Joe
sleep in their room
and John in his. I
think I'll make more toast.
—James Schuyler, from *Collected Poems* (Farrar, Straus and Giroux, 1993)

Notice the short lines—it's as if he were sitting staring out the window at the breakfast table with a small notebook. In fact he was. Just thinking out loud, on paper.

Write right now

Do the same. Sit for 5 minutes and just write what you see, whatever you're thinking, your hopes, prayers, dreams. Construe them together like stream of consciousness, as if recording a time capsule, or writing a thank you note. Write right now

JANE HERTENSTEIN

Hot Flash: Working In Series

What is a Series?

Simply put, it is a group of pieces based on a common element or group of elements. You can base a series on subject matter, a technique, a particular set of materials, a group of visual elements, or a compositional format. A series can be created in an afternoon—as in a group of quick collage studies—or last a lifetime. Many artists keep several series going throughout their careers.

- Working in series allows you to explore ideas more thoroughly, give them some breathing room.
- Working in series gives you the opportunity to try out different solutions to visual "problems", and explore multiple possibilities.
- Working in series gives your art practice focus and momentum. Rather than face the blank canvas with too many possibilities to choose from, the parameters of your series create clarity of intention.
- By considering the *series* the basic unit of art making, you lose the preciousness of the individual piece, the fear of "ruining" it, which can keep you stuck. Get unstuck by working in multiples.
- Committing to a quantity of pieces allows you to push through blocks and discover new solutions.

FROM http://janedaviesstudios.com/working-in-series/[24]

When I was in Washington DC in October 2015 I visited the National Gallery where there was an itinerate exhibit, *The Serial Impulse*. Let's face it, a series of anything is boring. I was about to skip and rush on to other things. But then, I thought, what is the art behind series? Warhol with his screen printing and Jasper Johns with his flag series. Van Gogh with his sunflowers and bedroom. Jane Freilicher revisited her subjects over and over again—pansies and peonies—she considered it a form of contemplation, meditation. The challenge isn't in the product but in the exercise, not in simply recreating as close to

---

24.   http://janedaviesstudios.com/working-in-series/

the original form, but to explore through process, to rediscover, to see anew after over-seeing. It's what happens after we are forced to play a piece over and over, after a while we become numb to it, it becomes abstracted, then after perhaps the 100th viewing, screening, listening, we have a breakthrough and begin to see, hear, feel differently about it.

From the National Gallery, *The Serial Impulse*:

Overview: For centuries artists have made multi-part series, undertaking subjects on a scale not possible in a single work. This engagement was especially prevalent in the 1960s, as artists dedicated to conceptual, minimalist, and pop approaches explored the potential of serial procedures and structures.

Write right now

For this Hot Flash—try working in a series. Pick something and see how many memories you can squeeze from each "topic."

*playgrounds

*ice cream stand

*drive-in movies

Here is a sampling of my series on Parking Lots:

Parking Lots #1

I remember standing in a parking lot saying goodbye not knowing if I'd ever see my friends again. After college time and money were like chains squeezing me tighter and tighter. I had to work, and travel was unpredictable. I couldn't rely on my car to get across town let alone across two states to come visit. If I even had the money for gas.

We were all on the brink of change. No one knew where they'd be in a year. What once seemed forever was an illusion, even illusions seemed transitory. Quicksand was all around us. We held on tight as we hugged each other good bye.

Years later when we reunited we were no longer the same people.

Parking Lots #2

We'd had another argument and so I went for a walk after dinner. It was dark, but darkness is only relative in the city. There is light everywhere. The atmosphere around the arc lamps sends diffused halos rippling out to the blurry edges. I walked along the shore of Lake Michigan and then through the bird sanctuary where everything was silent; from across the harbor came the muffled strum of auto traffic on the Drive. Popping out of the Magic Hedge and about to cross the parking lot, I spied a coyote silhouetted, the bristled hairs on his back standing up. He turned to look at me, the only two figures on an asphalt landscape. After a minute he galloped off and I continued circumnavigating the promenade before turning toward home.

Parking Lots #5

If I travel far back in time I am able to observe dinosaurs. Sometime around age five I went with my parents in the car to a fiberglass dinosaur exhibit in a shopping center parking lot. They were huge—bigger than a kindergartner! —on flatbed trucks. I remember their automaton necks wagging, a flash of plastic teeth, the flip of a tail. I riddled my parents with questions: Are they still around? How long ago did they die out? Were they really this big? What did they eat?

They were the most majestic thing I'd ever seen, and later, whenever passing that shopping center, I'd scan the parking lot for remnants of dinosaurs.

Hot Flash: Anne Porter, once and this is

I've been reading the poems of Anne Porter. Her first collection, *An Altogether Different Language* (1994), published when she was 83, was named a finalist for the National Book Award. Her other volume of poetry is *Living Things: Collected Poems* (2006).

I was struck upon beginning this collection how many of her poems seem to be reminiscences. Indeed, she lived a long life, passing away in 2011 just shy of her 100th birthday. A number of her poems begin with the word *once*.

The Wingéd Children
Once when my friends
Were driving through the desert
In Mexico
They passed a pickup truck
And in the back of it
Each with a pair of wings
Of sky-blue plush
Such as is used
For making bedroom-slippers
There rode a dozen little
Mexican children.

In addition she began a series of poems with *This is*.

Summer Cottage
This is a house
That smells of melons and roses
Sea-wind pours through it
The airy curtains float
And the wiry sprays
Of the sea-lavender
Tremble on the table
The hushed roar

Of the massive ocean
Covers us night and day
It shelters us
Like a tree shadow
We live in it
As in a forest.

(photo from Just Breath website)

Her simple language bestows a haiku hush. Her subject matter is mostly ordinary, domestic: her children (she had five), her home, her faith (a late convert to Catholicism). Her work exudes a humility, a selflessness. So that even though she writes about the tangible, she is at the same time revealing another dimension, something beyond this world. This is a collection filled with vignettes, haiku-like thoughts, remembrances, odes, and tributes to others.

Write right now

Begin by using the word *once*
Work on another piece with the zen-like *this is.*

JANE HERTENSTEIN

Hot Flash: Once Upon a Time

Many of us are used to the trope: Once upon a time . . .

That is how fairy tales or any spontaneous tale begins to unfold. Sometimes all one has to say is, *Once upon a time*—and the tale will spin itself. I once upon a time began a series or travel vignettes or flashes by imagining, remembering once upon a time.

Goreme, Turkey

One time we took a night bus from Selçuk to Goreme, better known as Cappadocia. Just like nomads traveling by night we'd come upon an oasis in the darkness where a squadron of attendants ran out to gas and wash down the exterior of the bus before we moved on into a vacuum. Eventually we arrived in town before sun up. We still didn't know exactly where we were. That's how it is with travel—especially in places with little doodley hooks on their letters; I was continually lost, unsure how to pronounce words, what to order to eat, afraid I wouldn't see the right stuff. Somehow we managed to make it to our hostel[25].

It was early; not a thing was stirring except a cat lounging on a cushion in the unlocked reception office. There was a computer there and I checked my email—though once again I was flummoxed by the foreign keyboard. Nothing was where it should be. I wandered outside. The sky was beginning to lighten, stars were growing dim. Slowly I became aware of shapes.

I remember feeling awestruck in sudden light as I realized I was standing in a courtyard surrounded by sand cave rooms carved out of unusually soft volcanic rock. It was like no place I've ever been.

---

25.   http://www.shoestringcave.com/

Write right now

Why not begin a flash or give yourself permission to flash by beginning with Once upon a time . . . or if too literal, remember back to once upon a time.

JANE HERTENSTEIN

Hot Flash: Abandoned Spaces

I've mentioned certain websites that can help to spark flashes. Abandoned Spaces[26] viscerally calls up nostalgic curiosity. I am always intrigued by the various spaces, once inhabited but now abandoned and the various relics left behind. I signed up for Facebook notifications so whenever there is a new post it shows up in my feed. I love the pictures and they motivate me to flash and write about memories.

From Abandoned Spaces website
The abandoned Helmsley Castle, Yorkshire, England

---

26.   https://www.facebook.com/Abandoned-Spaces-1631626090400340/

Sometimes it is a shoe store still warehousing and displaying styles from the 60s, sometimes it is a schoolroom from Chernobyl with decaying textbooks fertilizing a tree growing up between broken desks. Who isn't fascinated by ruins? They call to us, remind us that we are all mortal, that nothing stays the same, but will eventually breakdown, go back to nature. Even notions of religion—how many hollowed out churches and abbeys are there? In Turkey we toured grottos and underground Christian churches that are now archaic, in Rome we visited huge basilicas built upon the foundation of pagan temples, what was in suddenly becomes passé. Or, in the true style of history, wait long enough and the pendulum swings back; it is cyclical.

Nevertheless, we are drawn to these spaces. Here in the U.S., Detroit is now a major tourist stop for people who are curious about modern-day ruins. Friends of mine travel to Gary, IN to explore and take pictures at abandoned buildings, business sites.

Looking at these pictures stirs something up inside of me, causes me to think long and hard about what was, what might be, and who we could become.

Write right now

Pull out a box of old photos, write a caption, begin a memory, call up your sister, brother, friend, write about the day they took that picture, or what you recall of that place and what went on there.

JANE HERTENSTEIN

Hot Flash: Sketches

I stumbled upon an old copy of *Country Byways* by Sarah Orne Jewett published 1881. I'd read a long time ago *Country of the Pointed Firs* so I was familiar with Jewett. She has a very interesting personal history and is recognized as an outstanding regional writer, though lately her work has not received a lot of interest. *Byways* according to Wiki is described as "sketches."

Again, I was familiar with this term. Louisa May Alcott wrote *Hospital Sketches* (1863) about her experience working as a Union nurse during the Civil War. Her literary hero, Charles Dickens wrote *Sketches by Boz* (1839). Sketches to me seem like an early form of blog posts. From Wiki: A sketch story, literary sketch or simply sketch, is a piece of writing that is generally shorter than a short story, and contains very little, if any, plot. The genre was invented in the 16th century in England, as a result of increasing public interest in realistic depictions of "exotic" locales. A sketch story is a hybrid form. It may contain little or no plot, instead describing impressions of people or places, and is often informal in tone.

Write right now

Why not attempt a sketch, your impressions. Compose an impressionistic scene, a loose rendition of a recent experience or memory, or a quick jot from your travels.

Just now I am making up a book which is to come out in the fall—called Country By-Ways. It is mostly sketches of country life—and of my own country life. So far I have simply tried to write down pictures of what I see—but by and by I am going to say some things I have thought about those pictures. I don't know whether the pictures or the meditations will seem truest, but I know that I have found out some bits of truth for myself—

FLASH MEMOIR: WRITING PROMPTS TO GET YOU FLASHING

Letter from Sarah Orne Jewett to Theophilus Parsons, 12 June 1881

Right now, write!

Hot Flash: Write a Flash Mystery

Flash is a form that can be applied to almost any genre—not just fiction and memoir. At the Chicago Printer's Row book festival there was once an event judged by a panel of mystery novelists called Flash Mystery. Little mysteries that could be read and solved in under 3 minutes!

I've also heard them referred to as flash bang! Flash bangs are a type of contusion grenade meant to flush an assailant out of hiding or from shelter. They startle.

Flash is typically anything under 1000 words. Start small—the hardest challenge—by attempting a tweet mystery of 140 characters, and grow it, adding different word counts, 50, 100, etc. You basically have enough time to set it up, like a joke (or murder), and then get to the punchline, solution to the puzzle.

Write right now

Write a sudden mystery, a flash bang that will leave the reader startled. There are several places that accept flash bang, flash crime, or/and flash mysteries. https://flashbangcontest.wordpress.com/
http://flashbangmysteries.com/submissions/

Hot Flash: Clearing TSA

The 50-word challenge: bite-sized fiction everyday! http://fiftywordstories.com[27]/ was started in February 2009 by Tim Sevenhuysen. The goal was to post a 50-word story EVERDAY for one year. The rest is history—he's still going. With a little help from reader submissions.

What is a 50-Word Story?

From the website: A 50-word story is a piece of fiction written in exactly 50 words. That doesn't mean "roughly" 50 words; it doesn't mean "as close to 50 words as possible"; it doesn't mean 50 words or fewer. It means exactly 50 words.

As with any other form of fiction, a 50-word story should have a beginning and an end, a plot and character development (even if they are only implied), and a theme, meaning, or purpose of some sort. Many 50-word stories are built around twists or climactic moments.

So why not set yourself a 50-word challenge and write EVERYDAY about something EVERYDAY, aka ordinary.

Write right now

And, since this book is about inciting, giving a poke to our memories, why not write about Clearing TSA. What's this like for you? Is there pent-up anxiety followed by instant relief? What do you think about whilst standing in line? What could possible go wrong?

I picked Clearing TSA because it is something we have ALL gone through—as opposed to childbirth, winning a $902 million dollar lottery, etc. We've all queued up shoeless to expose our underwear, our carry-on, or toiletries in zip-loc baggies. What was your

---

27.   http://fiftywordstories.com/

Hot Flash: Frozen Chosen

Have you written any 50-word memoirs lately?

Perhaps you're frustrated because so much of life is not memorable. Basically we live ordinary lives. That's why many of my prompts are mundane. As writers we are meant to dig down, dig deep, to an inner core. A memory which on the surface seems rather anecdotal can often lead to some deeper meaning, a hidden truth.

the local truck stop

ordering a stack of silver dollar pancakes the biggest belly laugh

—or the fact that you passed a wreck on the highway

Write right now

Today's prompt is: Frozen Food Aisle. That's it. What is the story? What bubbles to the surface? What about those foggy doors after you've rooted around inside. How long have you stood and studied the individual flavors of ice cream, wishing life could be as varied and exciting? What does the frozen food aisle tell you about yourself?

Maybe it's where you met your mate.

Or where you first considered going for your MFA. Get inspired.

Hot Flash: Pain + Time

I was listening to an interview on Fresh Air with Garry Marshall (re-aired since he passed away) about his career writing comedy for TV and movies. He is best known for developing and writing for *Happy Days* among others. He said something interesting: time + pain=comedy.

We're always looking for that elusive creative spark.

Sometimes it is simply butt in chair. Sitting down and writing. Spending time with your material. This is not sexy advice. We always wish for the "secret," the inside scoop, the magic formula.

But often it comes with a prosaic thud. Live life, write about life. That's it.

He said when looking for material he would often remember back to an embarrassing moment. For instance, as a boy he refused to take his shirt off at the beach because one time his mother said you have so many moles, I bet I can connect the dots. Thereafter he was self-conscious about his moles and freckles. Later he would turn this into a famous episode on the *Dick Van Dyke Show*, the one where Rob falls asleep on the couch and his son (Ritchie?) comes in and connects the dots with an ink pen. Laura discovers that Rob's freckles form a facsimile of the Liberty Bell. He ends up appearing on a "reality" TV show, "Odd But True." http://www.hulu.com/watch/114020

This is exactly what I say in my flash memoir seminars: mine memories from your own life. Riff on stuff from your childhood, and sometimes the pain from the past becomes your most compelling material.

Let's look at an example. A detail became the basis for a short short, 100-word flash. A woman slipping her cellphone into her bra. I took that thought and crafted/flashed a piece called "Granny's Pockets" about someone who grew up referring to boobs as pockets because her grandmother was constantly tucking things away down the front of her dress. I wrote it, researched 100-word story journals, submitted the piece, had it accepted, and ONLINE[28] within a few hours. Really. http://www.fridayflashfiction.com/100-word-stories/grannys-pockets-by-jane-[29] hertenstein[30]

That was a record and gave me a real boost. (I boast.)

Granny's Pockets, by Jane Hertenstein[31]

I grew up thinking pockets were boobs. My granny had an ingenious way of carrying random objects; she'd tuck stuff down the front of her baggy dress into a fathomless well of cleavage. She kept things in her "pockets," her bra handier than any backpack. I once saw her produce a pair of scissors. I imagined things getting lost and surfacing years later. When the ice cream man came down the street, she'd reach inside and retrieve a sweaty coin purse, money jingling with every bounce. Even today I get confused. If caught without a purse, I'll always have pockets.

Write right now

Right now write a flash based upon some fledgling memory from your childhood, suppressed pain, the stuff of nightmares, and turn it into a narrative. Your most embarrassing moment.

Revisiting these memories might make for horror, comedy, or slice-of-life- anecdotal flash. Give it a try.

---

28.   http://www.fridayflashfiction.com/100-word-stories/grannys-pockets-by-jane-hertenstein

29.   http://www.fridayflashfiction.com/100-word-stories/grannys-pockets-by-jane-hertenstein

30.   http://www.fridayflashfiction.com/100-word-stories/grannys-pockets-by-jane-hertenstein

31. http://www.fridayflashfiction.com/100-word-stories/grannys-pockets-by-jane-hertenstein

Hot Flash: Unreliable Dust

Jane and I have been friends for over 40 years (of course, we were infants when we met). We often tag-team each other at Facebook and email. Most of it is innuendo, only to be understood by us, between us. Like a secret language, twin talk.

One day I had this idea: a collaborative letter. I wrote her, When did we first meet?

ME:

I believe I first met my friend Jane at a Young Life event downtown, in the city. If one can imagine: the idea of downtown Dayton sounding cool, exciting, the high life. I couldn't wait to attend. It would start at the YMCA pool and perhaps end at Chris' (the college-age women's leader) house for an overnight. I think we were also planning on having a late-night treat at Frisch's Big Boy Restaurant. They had a hot fudge brownie cake to die for.

I remember doing baby laps in a half-size pool the temperature of Nome, Alaska and being introduced to "another" Jane. I knew there must be others out there. Little did we realize we were about to embark upon a lifetime of friendship.

Forty years ago.

JANE (the other one):

Wow. You may be combining a couple of memories. There was a Young Life lock-in at the Y, at about that time. I was miserable. I guess those things are fun for teens who like to, you know, socialize. Chris absolutely was key. She "discipled" or "trained" us for work crew and it seems like we spent a lot of time with her. Hot fudge sundaes may have been involved. I remember being at a campaigners weekend retreat with you. Up in central Ohio? And Bob -—was working the weekend as staff. Was that our senior year? Maybe in the fall? I remember you asking if he was my boyfriend even though we weren't dating at the time. Maybe you and I were introduced at the lock-in. How did we get chosen for work crew? I'm glad for that work crew time—I think that in some ways, it changed my life a bit. Solidified some spiritual stuff anyway. Do I remember you from the coffeehouse on Saturday nights? What was it called? The Rock? I think I just put two and two together after I met you and saw your name on the prayer list. Memories rise like dust. Unreliable dust!

Write right now

Write a collaborative letter. Use the technology of Facebook, email, or even a phone call to work on a flash about how you met your best friend, mate, spouse, cousin's boyfriend's son- in-law. What do you remember, what do they remember, and put the two side-by-side to see the difference in recall and perception.

Hot Flash: Collaborative Letter

We used to write letters. Who knew that one day the act/art of letter-writing would disappear? I'm so glad I kept a few, stuck between pages of books and largely forgotten. After discovering one of these letters I wrote a flash memoir.

A Whole New Recipe

To Jane Jarrell McSweeney

The other day I discovered a letter you wrote to me dated 8/6/83. It was slipped into the pages of an old cookbook. What was I doing thirty years ago—making gravy?

You had just gotten married and were expecting a baby. I was still single. "Where does the time go?" you asked in the opening line. Your dad recently retired. That's when your dad was still living as was mine. Before the fragile brittleness of mortality entered in.

You say you'd love to come to Chicago, but your husband has a new job and can't get away. In Lima, Ohio. "Well," you write, "you have to start somewhere."

We'd become friends while freshmen in high school. Different schools. I still cannot remember the exact circumstances, but it involved Young Life and meetings with guitars and exuberant singing. "It Only Takes a Spark to Get a Fire Going." We ended up sitting next to each other and at one point in the song you turn to the person next to you and "pass it on." The summer before tenth grade we volunteered to work at a Young Life camp in the hills outside of Pittsburgh, PA for inner-city youth.

In your letter you mention people we met at camp and continued to hang with through college. Different colleges. You attended Ohio State and I went to OU (Ohio University). "Terri—should deliver her twins any day now!" "Yesterday was Mark—birthday," you remind me. All people I only have a tenuous grasp of who they are today.

"How are things for you?" you ask. "How's your summer so far?"

If I remember correctly I was trying to figure out what life was all about. After graduating from college and failing miserably to find a job, I'd come to Chicago to join a commune. I know—not exactly what I was originally thinking either. But as things turned out, the lifestyle appealed to me. Filled a few holes left by a dysfunctional family. Which, by the way, in your letter, you questioned my decision to skip a visit home. "I understand your parents kind of nag on you, but Jane I'm sure they love you." In retrospect your encouragement now sounds sort of sweet and naïve.

"Pray for me." You confess you are missing college, your family, all the people you were used to surrounding yourself with. "I just need a friend!"

I fold the letter and return it to its place in the cookbook. You were just here a few weeks ago visiting. The last time I saw you was ten years ago. And before that, maybe ten more years. Yet, even with the passing of time and living half a continent apart, we are still friends. We're still passing it on.

Write right now

Do you have old letters tucked away? Inside books? Safe deposit boxes?

Right now, reread an old letter and flash. What memories does this letter bring up? How would you reply today, many years hence?

Hot Flash: Recipe Memoir

Lately I've been reading about "borrowed" forms. There has been a recent explosion in creative nonfiction with writers employing hybrid forms, where essays borrow their structures from extra-literary sources (a recipe, a police or medical lab report, a pack of cards, an obituary...) to use as a framework for a meditation on the chosen subject. In the best examples, the borrowed structures are less contrived than inevitable, managing not only to give shape to the work but to illuminate and exemplify its subject.

Here is an interesting example, a story from the *Bellingham Review*. I remember as a kid reading *The Ladies Home Journal*, "Can this Marriage Be Saved?" Why? I mean, I was a kid. But for some reason, I found hope in the idea that nothing was beyond fixing. That no relationship was too broken. This should give readers insight into my psyche and troubled childhood! The following "borrowed" form piece is "Can This Troubled Marriage Be Saved: A Quiz"[32] by Nancy McCabe.

I've written earlier about the five senses and how they are immediate portals to memories. The memory of taste (along with sight) can lead us back. Proust's memory was suddenly inflamed by madeleines, a French cookie.

So what are these madeleines which inspired the Master of Memoir?

I had a French visitor who insisted on making madeleines. I watched her. The ingredients are fairly basic: butter, sugar, flour. The revered madeleine is a simple, ordinary butter cookie. Far less exciting than what I had imagined!

Sometimes a recipe causes us to remember—the people who handed it down to us, where we were when we made it, all the picnics or special suppers when we sat around a table and enjoyed a meal.

---

32.   http://bhreview.org/2011/10/11/can-this-troubled-marriage-be-saved-a-quiz/

Mom's Cranberry Relish
Thanksgiving always stirs up a lot of memories. And one memory I had over Thanksgiving—actually people kept reminding me—was my mother's cranberry relish recipe.

about 5 cups whole cranberries

start with 1 cup sugar, but you'll definitely be adding more
and 1 WHOLE orange, the whole thing

I remember when I called Mom to ask for it—she made a point of saying, the *whole* orange. But I usually cut it up just to check for seeds and make sure that pimply thing on one end has been removed.

Way back when, before what we now call a food processor, Mom had a huge kitchen contraption made out of die-cast metal and weighing about 50 pounds that did almost everything. It was like a wood chipper. A WHOLE orange was nothing for this baby. It could juice a rock. She had attachments she'd put on—like she used to make her own goose liver pâté. The thing actually had more attachments than her ElectroLux vacuum cleaner another heavy-duty appliance. They were all made out of old tank parts I believe.

She'd dump in the cranberries. Shhrrrr. Then the WHOLE orange. Shhhrrrr. Then more sugar than you might think—to tone down the bitterness of the cranberries and that orange peel.

That's it. No cooking, and not a lot of fuss.

Write right now

Cook up a recipe memoir. Is there a family recipe? Handed down through time that defies modern technology and Cuisinart? Is there something that calls forth inside of you a delicious memory.

Ready, begin, stir!

JANE HERTENSTEIN

Hot Flash: First Friend that Died

When you reach a certain age you start losing people. There's been a tally at the end of every year. 2016 reached new lows, new depths of grief. I've been thinking especially, somewhat retroactively as it happened during a very busy and then emotionally-occupying time, about my friend Curt Mortimer and all that he has meant to me through the years. His lifetime of selfless giving.

Checklist Before Dying:

*write a poem

*vote for Hillary

*watch an epic sunset

*drink a good cup of coffee (especially good if accompanied by a friend)

Curt had a check in every box before passing away on Election Day 2016 sitting on a park bench late afternoon. He is an example of someone who lived a good, long life committed to the people he loved.

But, I'm also reminded of the first person, the first friend I had that died. They weren't as lucky to have lived a good, long life. I remember the shock—of mortality, that time isn't forever, that we can be too late to right wrongs, to say we're sorry, to start over. Time ran out for Cheryl, for me.

She was a few years older than me. Her family had just moved to Centerville and were fundamentalist Christian. They believed in the healing power of God. So that when Cheryl was diagnosed with Hodgkin's leukemia they attempted prayer first.

Looking back there were a number of red flags.

Cheryl was their first born, the other siblings after her were blessed with athletic prowess, good looks, excellent singing voices (for all those gospel songs), and blind faith. Cheryl's faith, though rigid, allowed for grace. All she wanted was to be loved.

Even as a teenager I could see there were breaks—she was different, not like others, and her family seemed to ostracize her. I'm not sure they gave her a chance. She confessed to me once that she always felt like a sinner around them—especially her father. He was a hard man to please.

Back then I reckoned this was what we all felt—our families can be our own worse enemies. In this case, they actually were.

Cheryl fell in love and moved in with a boy about the same time she got her diagnosis. Together they worked in his father's doughnut shop. One day I got a phone call from her. (By this time I was a freshman in college in Dayton,) She asked if I could take her to her chemo treatment.

This seemed sort of odd and sad. She explained that her family wanted nothing more to do with her. That her boyfriend needed to work, so she was stuck. I thought it was because Cheryl never learned to drive. Because of a lack of self-confidence she never got a license or finished high school. But the real reason—I was to find out. I took her and came back for her, where upon she immediately threw up in my car. I learned that people on chemo shouldn't drive after a treatment. I got her home and upstairs into bed. She thanked me, but I sort of blew it off. I was confused about all the weird Christian logic. Was Cheryl so wrong to be left alone in this obvious time of need? I couldn't make sense of it.

But life went on and a few months later I heard she'd died. I was not expecting that. I have always thought back with regret: I should have done more, been more supportive, been a true friend. I know I could have done more for her, but ran out of time.

Write right now

What about you—is there someone from your past, your childhood, growing up years where their death struck you? Where perhaps their death spelled the end to childhood innocence, clued you in to your own mortality? Grandma, grandpa, great aunt? Write about the first peer or contemporary to die—and how it impacted your own life?

Hot Flash: List Memoir, part 1

I wrote earlier about borrowed forms. A list memoir is one such form. Maggie Nelson constructed a whole memoir based upon the color **blue**. The color acted as a footnote to her life, so it was visually set up as numbered sequences.

I did the same thing with :

100 Things Women Writers Should Consider[33] Originally appeared in *Minolta Review*

1. I write my friend: Should I give myself away, for free?
2. Why do I feel so bad for saying no? Guilty, as if free-fall blame will crush me.
3. How can I make you happy? By giving myself away. Asking nothing in return.
4. The director of Chicago Publishing Resource Center emails: Can you do a workshop this coming November? I ask about remuneration. We are a non-profit, he responds. We cannot afford to pay you.
5. I "sell" my work. It is free content.
6. As I struggle with self-identity: Am I a writer or am I a content provider? I want to make you happy.
7. But what about me? Am I happy?
8. On my tax returns under profession I put writer. Yet I am technically a non-profit.
9. Can I actually call myself a writer?
10. I tell people I write for the web. They nod.
11. What does this mean?
12. That, yes, legitimately I am leaving a digital footprint. That in a cyber bank I have a cache of words.
13. Yet I am poor. My confidence bankrupt.

---

33.   https://www.minolareview.com/jane-hertenstein

14. I email ChiPac: I need to know what you mean by stipend.

15. It depends.

16. So much depends upon title, description, and turnout. And, I muse: Gender?

17. What if I were a man?

18. Would a man even have to ask? Would a man give himself away for free?

19. I ask myself this as I work my other day job—frying eggs and flipping pancakes.

20. While standing at the grill I jot down story ideas on scraps of parchment paper used to line huge sheet trays.

21. Order up!

22. On my break I write in this notebook. No one ever asks: What is she doing?

23. How do I counteract this feeling that I am invisible?

24. Even my husband has stopped seeing me.

25. For our anniversary we went out with another couple. When the food arrived we dug in. Across from me I noticed my friend's partner had stopped talking. He was turning blue.

26. I've often struggled with giving up. Why? Why? Why?

27. But I always return to the question: What else would I do?

28. He's choking! I jump up and perform the Heimlich in the middle of the restaurant.

29. It's messy, but necessary.

30. Later, perhaps out of embarrassment, the couple never calls, never reciprocates with their own invitation. Suddenly they drop off the social radar.

31. I contemplate writing about this, always coming back to how? Why? What?

32. Afterwards, on the bus ride home, my husband laments: Someone should have helped him. What? I ask. He obviously was struggling, someone should have helped.

33. I remember when I put my hand on his back at the restaurant—the man was scared. I could see it in his eyes—wide behind spectacles. *He thinks he is dying.*

34. Someone did help.

35. Through his shirt and sweater, his heart beating, pounding into my palm.

36. Did you not see me standing over him? My hand on his back? Calling waitstaff, pushing, pounding? The vomit and then release?

37. I finally realize I am invisible to my husband.

38. ChiPac to me: Can I work on spec?

39. What does this mean?

40. For publishing cred. A by-line. Something to put in my CV.

41. The last royalty check I received was 15 years ago. It was negative. I never earned out my advance.

42. Yet what is art worth?

43. I pass the order thru the pass-thru window. A #7 over easy.

44. I can barely pay my bills between freelance and cooking. I pick over the bones.

45. A rag picker.

46. I should be grateful.

47. To work for free.

48. I leave my husband.

49. Whoever said something is better than nothing is stupid.

50. Sad. Lonely. Empty.

51. So I ask: Can you pay me something?

52. But what I'm really wondering is: What am I worth?

53. No one can tell me. I have to see it for myself.

54. I think of Louisa May Alcott whose character in *Little Women* cries out as if in pain: I hate being poor!

55. Even the title: *Little Women*

56. Today they'd be called girls, bitches, maybe sluts.

57. Louisa May Alcott through her writing became the sole supporter of her family.
58. Her earnings allowed her father Bronson Alcott to theorize about Transcendentalism.
59. I put my husband through grad school. He studied film theory.
60. And, all that hope, dreams of a future together are dashed.
61. Louisa loses her anchors, her mother and sisters.
62. She dies a spinster.
63. The fate of a great many female writers of that time period. Jane Austen, the younger Brontës, Emily Dickinson.
64. Without a patron or the support of a male editor (there was no other kind) Louisa would have perished.
65. She first submitted under a pen name meant to shield her true identity and give the impression she was a he.
66. Publishing was nasty business. You had to know someone. Many writers of the time turned to self-publishing. Dickens, Twain, Poe.
67. But what of the women writers? Could they take their future into their own hands?
68. George Sands, George Elliot, Isak Dinesen, S. E. Hinton, J. K. Rowling adopted male pseudonyms/personas when sending out manuscripts.
69. Catherine Nichols, if that is her real name, if we even believe her, did a query[34] experiment[35]. She submitted proposals under her real name and under a male pseudonym. Her male counterpart was 8 and a half times more likely to get a positive response from an agent, a request for a full, than Catherine received. Is this coincidence?
70. Google it to see what I'm talking about. She had to take

---

34. http://jezebel.com/homme-de-plume-what-i-learned-sending-my-novel-out-und-1720637627

35. http://jezebel.com/homme-de-plume-what-i-learned-sending-my-novel-out-und-1720637627

cover.

71. A safe place, a refuge.

72. I steal a moment in the walk-in cooler to put down words before they escape me. Should I give them away?

73. Starting out, it was fun. I wrote, I submitted, and the acceptances flew in.

74. I was paid in attention, accolades, affirmation.

75. But after a few years of this I wanted more.

76. Is it wrong to expect more?

77. So I made a decision: I would only submit to publications that pay.

78. Recently Jessica Piazza (I love her name!) has embarked on a project called Poetry[36] Has Value[37], a personal challenge to send more of her work to paying markets.

79. Google her. She is a terrific poet, deserving of pay, remuneration, a stipend, royalties, a grand prize.

80. She is the recent winner of the To the Lighthouse Poetry Prize[38]. Her winning manuscript is called: Interrobang from Red Hen Press[39], and also This is not a sky from[40] Black Lawrence Press[41].

81. A Room of Her Own.

82. First we must earn that room.

83. No one expects us to succeed. It's silly. Women have hobbies, men have jobs.

84. Poor Virginia Woolf walking into the river, her pockets full of stones.

---

36. http://poetryhasvalue.com/

37. http://poetryhasvalue.com/

38. http://aroomofherownfoundation.org/interview-with-jessica-piazza/

39. http://redhen.org/book/?uuid=FF0C9014-C558-0837-E311-A11304F24475

40. http://www.blacklawrence.com/this-is-not-a-sky/

41. http://www.blacklawrence.com/this-is-not-a-sky/

85. So where do we go from here?

86. What is possible?

87. No one knows for certain.

88. Publishing is changing. Journalism is dead. The *SunTimes* announces sweeping lay-offs. Former reporters are turning to blogging.

89. I work with one at the restaurant. Many writers have become waiters. Many waiters write.

90. We kvetch together, but nothing changes—except change.

91. We continue to submit in the hope

92. that someday someone will want us

93. because what else would we do.

94. That's not a question but a statement.

95. It is who we are, who I am.

96. Wrapped up in a thousand uncertainties, misapprehensions, against my better judgment.

97. Every once in a while

98. I

99. get

100. lucky.

Write right now

Write a list memoir. Start with #1 and let yourself go from there. What comes next? Freewheel from one thing to the next and see how they intersect on the page.

Hot Flash: List Memoir, part 2

A list poem is a combination of haiku and the prosaic list. It is an itemization but also a creative way of looking at something.

Here is an example from my own archives:

You know summer is over when

—snow piles up on window ACs. You know summer is over when

—all the swimming pools are empty hulls. You know summer is over when

—the streets glisten from icy rain. You know summer is over when

—you shiver stepping out of the shower. You know summer is over when

—even the dogs put on jackets. You know summer is over when

—the marigolds die.

You know summer is over when

—they bring the patio umbrella inside. You know summer is over when

—the mice run into the house. You know summer is over when

—Starbucks begins to advertise their Pumpkin Chai Latte. You know summer is over when

—the lake turns green beneath a slate gray sky.

Write right now

What is it you still need to do this summer, the bike rides, the grill outs, or the concerts in the park? Or the friends you need to meet up with? Write your own list.

Hot Flash: Hawaiian White Ginger

Did your Mom ever order from the Avon catalog? Remember the Avon lady? She came around door-to-door with brochures and samples (usually a neighbor trying to earn extra bucks). I always loved the Hawaiian White Ginger.

What is this fragrance? On-line it is described as containing notes of citruses, green grass, jasmine, rose and ginger. I'm not sure it's something found naturally in nature or was spawned in a laboratory. It's something only myself and a grandmotherly-type person would like. Thus this classic fragrance as well as the Avon lady have long been retired.

Yet just the other day I was reminded of this when an odor wafted by me. That smell! And immediately the rhythms of onomatopoeia, the surfboard balance of the words: Hawaiian White Ginger came over me. I remembered exactly what it was like to wear it and how it felt.

Comfortable, gracious, light and airy, like an exotic flower opening up on a dewy evening. All that in one whiff.

Write right now

Using your sense of smell, utilizing your sense of nostalgia, write about a smell that encapsulates your youth, something specific to an event in your past—or simply reminisce about the Avon lady, the homely woman you practically felt sorry for and ended up buying sacks of creams, lotions, and sprays that sat around in your bathroom vanity for years. Until you emptied out the house after Mom died. Go back, return to Hawaiian White

Hot Flash: Unmade Phone Calls

Many of my blog/Substack readers know that I am a fan of the New York School of Poets—which is not really a school at all! but a collection of friends who inspired and collaborated with each other. It even spawned a second-generation of poets—who really weren't a generation removed but only a few years younger. Trust me—these writers aren't anything like what you would expect!

Frank O'Hara said that many of his poems worked as unmade phone calls. This was back before social media. His poetry could be interpreted as missives to friends, ideas, thoughts he wanted to convey. They were often short, full of innuendo and shorthand that only those within his circle might truly understand. Sometimes Kenneth Koch might start a poem and then mail it to O'Hara who might in turn after adding some lines send it off to John Ashbery. And so on.

Our idea is to do something with language / That has never been done before / Obviously—otherwise it wouldn't be creation / We stick to it and now I am a little nostalgic / For our idea, we never speak of it any more, it's been / Absorbed into our work, and even our friendship / Is an old, rather fragile-looking thing.

Maybe poetry took the life out of both of them, / Idea and friendship.

—Kenneth Koch, "Days and Nights"

Frank O'Hara wrote poetry almost every day of his adult life. He would pause wherever he was to write a poem off the top of his head. Some of his most famous poems were written while he was on his lunch break or out for a walk. His small book *Lunch Poems* appears to have been composed primarily during his lunch break from his job at the Museum of Modern Art.

"A Step Away From Them" begins, "It's my lunch hour, so I go/ for a walk among the hum- colored/cabs." "Personal Poem" begins, "Now when I walk around at lunchtime/I have only two charms in my pocket." In the poem he mentions several friends: Mike Kanemitsu, LeRoi Jones, Miles Davis, and several other writers. He also references street signs and other familiar points, jazz joints in NYC: "I walk through the luminous humidity passing the House of Seagram," "get to Moriarty's where I wait for LeRoi," "last night outside of BIRDLAND." Toward the end of the poem, O'Hara wonders: "if one person in 8,0000,000 is thinking of me . . ."

Write right now

Pen an unmade phone call to someone, tell them what it is that you are thinking about, or what you wish with all your heart to communicate.

Hot Flash: Write Your Own Epitaph

Here is another example of a borrowed form.

An epitaph a short text honoring a deceased person. Technically it is inscribed on a tombstone or plaque. The essence of writing small. The original 6-word memoir,[42] the ultimate flash. Frank O'Hara's plaque at Green River Cemetery in a tiny graveyard in Springs, East Hampton ,reads:

Virginia Woolf (This quote is from the end of Woolf's novel The Waves, chosen by Leonard Woolf for the memorial plaque he put in their backyard.)

"Death is the enemy. Against you I will fling myself, unvanquished and unyielding o Death! The waves broke on the shore."

Poet, Charles Bukowski "Don't try."

Not as depressing as it seems: Bukowski explained the phrase in a 1963 letter to John William Corrington, writing "Somebody at one of these places ... asked me: 'What do you do? How do you write, create?' You don't, I told them. You don't try. That's very important: 'not' to try,

---

42.   http://www.sixwordmemoirs.com/

either for Cadillacs, creation or immortality. You wait, and if nothing happens, you wait some more. It's like a bug high on the wall. You wait for it to come to you. When it gets close enough you reach out, slap out and kill it. Or if you like its looks you make a pet out of it."

John Keats' last request was that he be buried under a blank tombstone with no name or date, only "Here lies one whose name was writ in water." His friends had other ideas and his tombstone bears another inscription—one that though flash is not exactly as short as what he asked for.

Write right now

This is an easy task, a flash you can write in your bathing suit sitting on a towel at the beach. Take a second or two to scribble down what you think you might be known for, what you want to leave behind, the last word.

Right now write, your own epitaph.

Hot Flash: Not Really a Unique Situation

Certain institutions are part of the fabric of our lives. Unique Thrift store has been part of my Chicago experience ever since I moved here in 1982. But, like a lot of things as we age, there are hard losses.

In 2016 Unique Thrift closed its doors.

The shop had recently undergone a brain-dead upgrade. I mean the whole reason people shopped there was to save money. Instead the new owners decided to make it into more of a boutique.

Less choice and higher prices. Please tell me—is this good sense?

In the thrift store market you need to overwhelm the customer with crap. So much of it that eventually you make money off of it. It used to be you could go into Unique on payday and come out with 3 – 4 grocery sacks of stuff and pay as little as $20. But that was a steady flow of money—until the upgrade. It was sad really, you'd go in and the aisles would be clear, the clothes arranged according to size (WTH!) not just color, and you could actually hear the Muzak. No more sloppy aisles with clothing getting tangled up in the wheels of your cart—ha, if you could score a cart. No more loud, crying children and mothers screaming SHUT YOUR ASS!

No more finding bras mixed in with the cutlery. Books (their biggest mistake) no longer priced at 10 cents to 50 for a hardback, now a dollar or 2. And for absolute dreck. Several times my husband and I would wander in after perhaps an old professor donated his entire library. Titles you seldom see except at higher-end resale shops or used bookstores.

Chalk it all up to the Internet, that fiend replacing all of us. Except who really wants to bother leaving their house when you can push a button and have a drone deliver it. Even CCO, the shelter where I volunteer, has both a physical store and an on-line presence. On-line sales now accounts for a 1/3 of their business.

The news was devastating, but it really hit the young people the hardest. So many friends' kids grew up with Unique that it is a bit like losing their innocence, like learning the hard lessons of life (and commerce). They are grieving as if they've lost a loved one.

Write right now

Growing up—you had many touchpoints, things you took for granted until one day they were no longer there. Sometimes this is the death of a parent or other close person, sometimes it divorce. As kids we are suddenly struck that behind that golden curtain there might not be a wizard. Things do change. Irrevocably. And, we have no control.

That's what hurts the most. The fact that some things cannot be fixed.

Right now write—what was that moment when the glasses came off, when you suddenly knew, when you grew up.

Hot Flash: The Crazy Stuff I Used to Do

It used to be that I jumped headfirst into every crazy thing. If someone came in the middle of the night and said we need you to go to the suburbs to rescue so and so, I wouldn't think twice but would pick up my purse. If someone needed driven to the hospital, I'd ask, "Do I have time to use the bathroom?" I can remember being asked to do a lot of crazy things.

That's why when I checked Facebook Saturday a.m. and saw that my daughter had posted about leaving her phone in an Uber, I knew my morning might not be lazy. She often works nights and takes a ride home instead of her bike.

Mid-morning she stopped in and I immediately asked if she'd gotten it back—no, but I know where it is. The iCloud had tracked her phone to the far northern suburbs. Without batting an eyelash I stood up and said, We're gonna go get it.

But first I'd have to borrow a car, since I don't have one. Not an Uber, though. A friend loaned us her van and we took off, tracking the phone to outside of Libertyville, where every village is called Round Lake, Grayslake, etc. We ended up outside of an apartment building.

There it is! We found the car, but when I rang her phone we realized it wasn't in the car. We'd have to find the driver—amongst one of the units in the building. We started with one where we could hear people moving around inside. A woman answered the door and Grace asked for Ahmed. She got her grandson to interpret for her since she only spoke Spanish. No.

We realized we'd have to knock on many more doors. I was starting to feel foolish for taking off on this hair-brained venture. We didn't really have a solid plan. Grace knocked on another door and a man in a bathrobe answered. Did I mention that in my advance state of second-guessing I began to think: We could be killed, cut up into tiny pieces, stuffed into a Dumpster. The usual train of thinking I used to have when off on an escapade—something along the lines like this might turn out really bad.

But it was Ahmed and yes he had her phone. He'd contacted Uber to let them know, but because Grace hadn't ordered the ride (her friend had) she didn't know who to contact and they didn't have her info either.

Success! But it yanked me back down memory lane. So that when I told an old friend about our adventure she said, Do you remember that time we went to check out a serial killer or some cult guy? I seriously did not remember. Are you making this up? No, she said, I'm pretty sure it was you—and all I could say was, well, it sounds like something I would do.

Now I've got to track down that story and write it up later.

Write right now

Write about the craziest thing you've ever done—or one of the many craziest things you've ever done.

Hot Flash: This Isn't Going To Turn Out Good

How many of us have had that feeling, that tickle inside your stomach, that your brakes have failed?

Let's just say as a kid growing up, a lot. I was constantly getting into trouble. Not shoplifting, skipping school, smoking behind the garden shed kind of trouble. More like smoking outside the fireworks factory.

I still remember sneaking out late at night to go on a motorcycle ride with my friend. He zipped me into a jumpsuit—in case we crashed, he said, I wouldn't lose the top layer of skin. Good thing, because we came to a sign at the bottom of a steep hill that as we flashed by it—my brain translated the letters: Bridge Out.

Write right now

Go ahead—tell us about the crazy, the craziest of crazy. Flash about the inkling you got before all hell broke loose, before the wheels came off. (The worst part is when your mother/mother/conscience asks: Why? There is no answer.)

Hot Flash: The Only Time I've Been Arrested

The only time I've ever been arrested . . . sounds like a good writing prompt.

The only time I've ever been arrested was about 40 years ago on an overpass in Nebraska.

I'd flown out from Dayton, Ohio to visit my sister working at a summer camp in Platte. It was the end of the season yet before time to go back to college. At that time in Ohio classes didn't start until the second half of September.

I remember the silty-bottom rivers and sand cranes, the sound of them calling to each other over the rolling hills. Outside of that and getting arrested there isn't much else I remember about Nebraska.

That summer a friend had introduced me to the thrill of sitting on an overpass above the highway and the rush when a semi passed beneath, the sudden whoosh as it flew out.

I'd sit with my feet dangling, feeling the aero dynamics through my thin-soled sneakers. Movies and bowling cost money, but this was free.

So on my last night in Nebraska I talked one of my sister's co-workers into going with me to a bridge. He was very enthusiastic. "Let me get some cookies." I'm sure I thought, Great idea! We might get hungry. Little did I suspect he was going to toss them off the bridge at the traffic down below.

At some point, I probably joined in.

We were just getting started when headlights turned off and a car came our way, onto the country road. We were skedaddling when the cop car pulled up. We were caught red-handed with cookies. The rest is hazy.

I know we were lectured on how dangerous it was to throw anything onto the highway.

I'm pretty sure we were sorry. Regardless, I and the other guy were taken in. I wasn't carrying any ID. The worse part was having to call my sister from the station. Or, maybe the worse part was the thought of missing my plane because I was in jail. I really, really wanted to get out of Platte.

Anyway, my sister showed up. I don't think she had to pay bail. We were released under our own recognizance, sent home with my sister who was still trying to process what exactly we'd been up to that evening. We made it back to the camp in time for me to pack and for my sister to drive me to the airport.

Write right now

How about you? Do you have a story to tell? Write a flash about that one time, the last time, the only time you've ever been arrested. Right now write.

JANE HERTENSTEIN

Hot Flash: Flash Nightmares

The other day I had a flash, a memory—and it still brings a chill over me. It's one of those nightmare memories, along the lines of standing next to your high school locker naked. I needed help moving and a friend loaned me his car—just one tiny problem: it was a stick shift. Like a normal twenty-year old, I thought this wasn't going to be a problem. I loaded up the vehicle and told myself, All I have to do is get out of first and I'm rolling. It took me an hour just to get out of the driveway.

On the roadway (I remember now it wasn't a highway, but a very busy divided road—much like Far Hills Ave.) all I wanted to do was cruise. Not have to stop for a red light. Which might have worked had I not had to go about 8 miles.

Eventually I did have to stop. I can still feel the terror come over me as I stalled out and, in my anxiety and fluster, was unable to get the car into gear. Either I would be rear-ended or towed, and none of these ideas appealed to me. I started, jerked, and tried again to figure out how to shift.

All around me cars were honking. I know, I know, I wanted to scream. Until at a certain point I realized drivers were also pointing, vigorously stabbing their fingers. Huh? I looked in the rear view mirror to see clothes and boxes strewn across the lanes. Ohhhhh.

I must've forgotten to close the hatch.

On a scale of one to ten, I was a twelve for stress that morning. I parked right there and got out and began gathering my things. Dashing here and there, collecting whatever I could.

I eventually made it to my new apartment and called the car's owner to come get it. I was in no shape to return it. Afterwards, I recall putting on a blouse that had tire marks on it, and reliving that moment, stuck in between gears.

Write right now

What's your go-to horror story? That moment you don't want to remember, but can't seem to forget.

Hot Flash: Halloween

I was reminiscing with someone in their thirties, (I know, What do they have to reminisce about?) but this person hit the nail on the old pumpkin head. Halloween has grown into a major American holiday. "When I was little it was just one day. Now my kids are sucked into harvest parties and activities for a whole month—not the least a whole weekend of unending trick or treating."

Growing up it was monumental to carve a pumpkin. Now suburban moms buy a station wagon full and put them everywhere for decorations. Trick or treating was one night only. And, we didn't drive around and hand-pick the best neighborhoods. We simply walked up and down the streets. We didn't spend half a year figuring out a novelty costume. I wore what my siblings had outgrown.

Ahh, simplicity.

Anyway, my friend took a garbage bag of random costumes to the Syrian refugees she's been visiting and mentoring. To say the least, the kids were beside themselves with excitement. I can't imagine fleeing war-torn Syria, barrel bombs, and food shortages—to end up in America, in Evanston going door-to-door where people HAND OUT FREE CANDY. How great is this place! Welcome to America!

Write right now

You must have a favorite Halloween memory—your first spook house, walking hand-in-hand with your dad, hanging out with your friends, or that moment when you realize you're too old to go trick or treating.

Hot Flash: Sinclair Dinosaur

Remember back in the day when certain detergents included benefits for the housewife—like a glass. Really you might be thinking—a glass? Somehow they didn't break, shards mixed in, shredding our clothes in the washer. There used to be all kinds of incentives or bonuses to purchases that had nothing to do with each other. Wash your clothes and drink a glass of wine!? It wasn't always Cracker Jacks that came with a prize inside, but also boxes of cereal. Not sure how big these boxes were but there would be books, airplanes to build, fannypacks, towels!!?? You used to be able to "collect" a whole set of tableware just by filling up at the gas station.

My Aunt Mart and Uncle Mike used to take me for a week or two in the summer. I loved being an only kid. After picking me up in Dayton to take me to Akron we'd stop for gas. At a Sinclair station they weren't giving away, but I think selling a Sinclair toy dinosaur, the kind you inflate. I knew better than to ask for one, but always coveted it when I saw them advertised on the signs. Uncle Mike came out of the station carrying one under his arm for me.

I thought it was the greatest thing ever. It stood about 2 feet high (or maybe that's the way I imagine it).

Write right now

So for any of you out there old enough to remember premiums or give-aways—write a flash. There's got to be something there, something hidden inside.

Hot Flash: Vintage Commercials

Who among us can attest to the power of advertising, the pervasiveness of an old commercial? There's a sub-channel on my TV list called Decades (there's also a channel that runs nothing but old game shows!). Anyway, for breaks in the *Bionic Man* and *Columbo* the station will air, in addition to current advertising, old commercials. A blast from the past. Instantly we are transported back. Friends via Facebook are constantly pointing me to YouTube favorite commercials from their childhood. It seems those annoying interruption s are now touchstones for some of us.

Whether the message succeeded in convincing us to buy or switch or consume, we are nevertheless under the spell. Images and words that continue to this day to influence us—woven into our collective memory.

There used to be an ad for Anacin[43] where an early 1960s housewife (really?) is in the kitchen and obviously under an enormous amount of stress. She snaps at her mother-in-law: "Mother I'd rather do it myself." I remember MAD magazine doing a parody (their best feature!) for a product called Anasprin.

---

43.   https://youtu.be/GshovE9F3F8

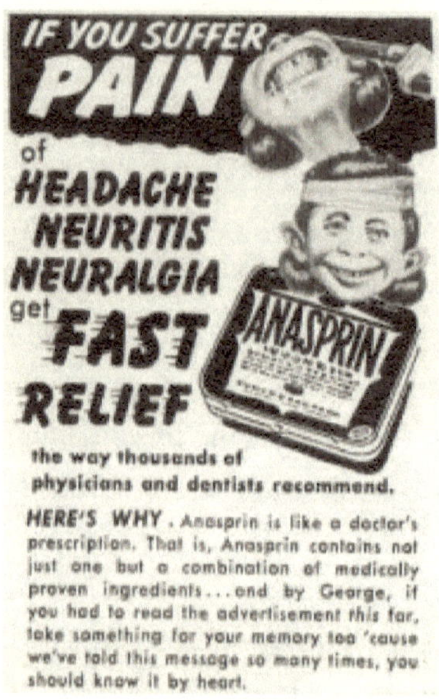

My memory trigger went off the other day when I was frying something. Looking down into the hot oil, which can sometimes also trigger my gut, I flashed an old commercial about Crisco oil not being greasy. Which is so ridiculous because isn't that the *very* nature of oil? Anyway the woman was interrupted when frying some chicken and turned off the heat under the skillet to attend to her child's broken arm. Once home from the emergency room she resumed frying, assuming the end product would taste greasy because of course it had sat half an afternoon in the vat of fat. (Now I know this is an old commercial because today they'd still be in the waiting room.)

Now just to be honest—both times I Googled to find the source, the vintage commercial I used the wrong brand name. For the headache medicine I first thought it was Excedrin and I searched first for Wesson oil. This also proves my point about the power of advertising—the message gets stuck in our memory and conversely corrupted.

Write right now

I'm sure all of us can recall a TV commercial from our youth. Use the power of advertising to recall and call forth and flash.

And, just to get you thinking, here's some vintage jingles: Ding dong — calling

Where's the — ? A little dab will —

Hey, Mabel — beer Just — it!

Like a good neighbor

What kind of kids eat — hotdogs? And, lastly, I wish I were an — wiener!

Hot Flash: Missed Connections

I've already written about using today's headlines as writing prompts. It's a trick I read first- hand from Frank O'Hara and his poem "Lana Turner has collapsed[44]." Comedians have long known the possibilities of mining the headlines for material. Meanwhile writers can gain inspiration from the news.

In a similar vein check out Craigslist. In Free Stuff alone are dozens of stories. Missed Connections is another area where stories can be harvested.

Cute lady working at the Bank on Milwaukee Ave

> We hit a great conversation about weather, travel and places we have visited. I thought you were very cute and had this awesome personality.
>
> I made a comment about your last name and then I said I have visited that country
>
> ... tell me the name of the country we were talking about. Seems like our conversation was cut short because of the limited time we had given the transaction and the number of people that were in line of course waiting. lol

No wonder I wait so long in line at the bank!

Some of the posts can be a little creepy (warning: weirdness abounds), while some are simply sad.

Emily

> Hey hope you are doing well. Think about you from time to time and wish we were friends. It sure would be nice to talk. Will you call me?

---

44.   https://www.poets.org/poetsorg/poem/poem-lana-turner-has-collapsed

God blessed the broken road

We met almost 12 years ago and dated for a bit before you moved home. You asked me to go with but I didn't. I think about you quite often, sometimes wondering what could have been? I'm probably shooting in the dark reaching out on here but I figured why not give it a shot. Tell me who you are, what my name is and what CD did we have on repeat all day every day pretty much.

Some are philosophical and some are poetic. They can be addicting, one leads to another. Many a story can be spun.

Write right now

Peruse Craigslist. Read through Missed Connections. Write your own Missed Connection— what would you like to say to that random stranger or to your friend from long ago. Flash a 50-word missive like an arrow sprung straight to the heart.

Hot Flash: Lost and Found, part 1

How many of you were captured by these headlines: **Woman interrupts concert to give the singer a bag of her possessions, taken from her tour truck in 1979**

That's right—someone gave Patti Smith her clothes back after 36 years.

This book is essentiallyabout memories. How many memories are stitched into the clothes we wear . . . or used to wear? The dress you wore to your son's wedding, your favorite sweatshirt that always gets rotated to the front of the drawer, the mini-skirt that got you through your darkest days after the breakup, that sheer blouse that always makes you feel ravishing, that hopelessly out-of-date tie that you somehow cannot bring yourself to forsake.

Who is it that said we are the clothes we wear?

But, styles change. Yesterday's punk is today's conservative. Remember your goth phase when everything you wore was black. I wouldn't be caught dead in an 80s dress with poof sleeves. The free bins are full of fuchsia jackets with padded shoulders.

Nevertheless, it isn't the style or even the fact that we once were skinny enough or bold enough to wear a certain item. It's about what it represents—that young renegade, that girl who never said no, but always YES!!!

Once I wore a thrift-store find, a beautiful paisley sari, over black leggings. I felt so beautiful and confident . . . until my husband and I had an argument. I never could bring myself to wear that sari again. I eventually sent it back to the thrift store with a sack of other things I no longer had a use for.

When Patti Smith was handed on stage a bag containing clothes stolen from her tour van in 1979, when she peek inside the bag, she was brought to tears.

Forget the numerous questions or the possible recrimination: she was flooded with memories of that 1979 kick-ass Patti. This Patti: (from *The Guardian*)

A clearly emotional Smith identified the top as the one she wore on the cover of Rolling Stone magazine in July 1978, and the cloth as belonging to her brother and road manager, Todd Smith, who died in 1994. Before long, half the audience was crying with her ... [Some] were asking where, how, why, but Patti just put her hands out and said she doesn't care how, she's just so grateful to have these priceless items back," a witness described in an online forum. "The rest of the program, after she piled everything on the podium, she couldn't stop touching them, eventually slowly slipping the bandana into her pocket . . and proceeded to do a ripping version of *Because the Night* with her son on acoustic guitar.

Write right now

Write a flash love letter to your favorite item of clothing.

JANE HERTENSTEIN

Hot Flash: Lost and Found, part 2

My last post was about a random bag of clothes close to 40 years old. Stuff no one wanted— except when they were returned to the former owner Patti Smith, she burst into tears. At the very thought, the clothes brought back profound memories.

Consider other infamous lost items. There is a history of art stolen through the ages, later recovered. The current controversy concerns art taken and stored in Nazi warehouses eventually winding its way back to the original owners. Or heirs. Museums are full of objects "taken."

I did some research and came up with stories of lost and found. Peter Frampton had an incident similar to Patti's while on tour. His plane crashed—and his equipment in the cargo bay, or so he thought.

Another mystery of a missing musical instrument solved: http://www.npr.org/2012/01/07/144799712/framptons-dream-guitar-recovered-decades-later

There's a group that does nothing but scour old battlefields for lost bones in the hopes of, through DNA testing, returning the remains of missing soldiers to their loved ones.

Even a few days ago I thought I'd lost a file I'd been working on. I must have mislabeled it and it ended up in a folder called temp on my desktop. I'm not even sure how I recovered it, but I lost no time in renaming it and putting it somewhere better for the next time I needed it.

Poor Hemingway, he didn't have the cloud. Or any other backup services. Really poor, poor Hadley. You see, she lost a valise containing every last piece of written work by her beloved husband.

It was 1922 and Hemingway was on the verge of a breakthrough. He'd been slaving away at his writing for months and months. He felt he was about to get a bite. Meanwhile he took a job filing a report for the Toronto Star as a foreign correspondent which took him away from Paris. And Hadley. After about a month he wrote to her to join him in

Geneva. All on her own she decided to empty Earnest's writing cabinet, even the carbon copies, and bring them with her on the train. It was her thought that Earnest could work on them during their holiday break. She stuffed them into a valise and left for the busy railstation.

We know this story does not end well. I cannot imagine what I would have done if I were Hadley—or Earnest Hemingway.

From *A Moveable Feast*:

"I had never seen anyone hurt by a thing other than death or unbearable suffering except Hadley when she told me about the things being gone. She had cried and cried and could not tell me. I told her that no matter what the dreadful thing was that had happened nothing could be that bad, and whatever it was, it was all right and not to worry. We could work it out. Then, finally, she told me. I was sure she could not have brought the carbons too and I hired someone to cover for me on my newspaper job. I was making good money then at journalism, and took the train for Paris. It was true alright and I remember what I did in the night after I let myself into the flat and found it was true."

Gone. All of it. All his Michigan Indian Camp stories. Every last shred.

Write right now

What if that valise hadn't been stolen? What if somehow today someone showed up on "Antiques Roadshow" with the aforesaid valise? Re-write history. http://www.thehemingwayproject.com/ hadley-talks-about-the-lost-manuscripts/

JANE HERTENSTEIN

Hot Flash: Lost and Found, part 3

Memoir today is being written as fiction and much of fiction is comprised of memoir. Flash is about writing small and using bits of your life story.

The Double Life of Liliane by Lily Tuck is essentially an autobiographical novel. Okay, there's a muddle. Which is it? Fiction or non-fiction.

Life is all about compartmentalizing. Except not everything fits. There are times when fact and fiction are indistinguishable from each other. This is a writer who is very familiar with historical fiction; she is the National Book Award winner of *The News From Paraguay*.

From my review:

"Tuck includes often segue into relevant historical information — about street names, for example, ocean liners, news stories of the day — lending an aura of even greater veracity. All of this is further backed up and given added authority by the inclusion of old photographs."

At times there is a point-by-point match between her life events and the narrative, then come the deviations. We're always rewriting the past. Seeing things through new eyes, another angle. Or to our benefit.

I know many of the things I write about in the first-person could be my story, but I've actually borrowed from someone else's life. Or I might re-cast my own history adopting a persona. We do this all the time. We're writers.

Write right now

Right now—write a flash memoir in less than a 1,000 words where you blend fact and fiction. Tell us what you *think* happened.

Acknowledgements

Unless specified all photos belong to Jane Hertenstein

The following pieces first appeared in:

"Centerville, Ohio" 2017, *Fiftywordstories*

"Sense of Smell" Spring 2012, *IMPACT: A Collection of Short Memoir*

"Young and Dumb" Summer 2009, *Flashquake*

"Granny's Pockets" Summer 2016, *Friday Flash Fiction*

"A Whole New Recipe" 2021, *Dove Tales*

"100 Things for Women Writers to Consider" Spring 2017, *Minola Review*

Jane Hertenstein is a Pushcart nominee and the author of a middle-grade novel, *Cloud of Witnesses* and YA novel, *Beyond Paradise*. Her non-fiction *Orphan Girl* was widely reviewed and featured in the *Chicago Tribune* Sunday Book Section. Her work has been recognized by the *New York Times*. She writes both macro and micro: fiction, creative non-fiction, and blurred genre. She's an alum of the Bread Loaf Writers' Conference waitstaff, Sewanee Writers' Conference, and the Amanda Davis Award, Wesleyan Writers' Conference. Jane is the recipient of multiple grants from the Illinois Arts Council and City of Chicago. Every year she rides her bike hundreds of miles and currently resides in the piney woods of Michigan. She teaches a workshop on Flash Memoir and is available for speaking. Her website is www.janehertenstein.com[45] and she can be found blogging at www.memoirouswrite.blogspot.com

Her life motto is Do Everything with your One Wild and Precious Life.

45.　　http://www.janehertenstein.com

"This is a lovely and helpful book. Sometimes just the right quote is all it takes to remind me that we writers are in this together–that it's hard for all of us, but that a writing life is a considered life and a terrific life. I came across a number of quotes in this book that I had never read before, almost all of them provocative and useful. I recommend this book to other writers to dip in and out of, for that little bit of inspiration and affirmation whenever you need it." Amazon Reviewer

Many of us are looking to write memories, either in the form of literary memoir or simply to record family history. This how-to book looks at memoir in small, bite-size pieces, helping the writer to isolate or freeze frame a moment and then distill it onto paper.

What readers are saying

"Just recommended this book to my memoir-writing friends. [Hertenstein] has freed me from the shackles of narrative and chronology."

"This resource is well-written, easy to follow, has concise and well-structured chapters, and lots of prompts to get a writer going. I highly recommend this book to anyone interested in writing flash memoir, or learning more about it."